I Found Love

My Journey of Hope, Perseverance, and Finding True Love

VERONICA BORNN

KP PUBLISHING COMPANY

Copyright 2020 by Veronica Bornn

All rights reserved. In accordance with the U.S. Copyright Act of 1976, the scanning, uploading, and electronic sharing of any part of this book without the permission of the publisher is unlawful piracy ad theft of the author's intellectual property. If you would like to use material from this book (other than for review purposes), prior written permission must be obtained by contacting the publisher at info@knowledgepowerinc.com

Thank you for your support of the author's rights.

ISBN: 978-1-950936-50-2 (Paperback)
ISBN: 978-1-950936-51-9 (Ebook)
Library of Congress Control Number: 2020914419

Editor: Frank Williams
Cover Design: Angie Ayala
Interior Design: Jennifer Houle
Literary Director: Sandra L. Slayton

Holy Bible, New Living Translation, copyright © 1996, 2004, 2007, 2013, 2015 by Tyndale House Foundation. Used by permission of Tyndale House Publishers Inc., Carol Stream, Illinois 60188. All rights reserved.

Scriptures taken from the Holy Bible, New International Version®, NIV®. Copyright © 1973, 1978, 1984, 2011 by Biblica, Inc.™ Used by permission of Zondervan. All rights reserved worldwide. www.zondervan.com The "NIV" and "New International Version" are trademarks registered in the United States Patent and Trademark Office by Biblica, Inc.™

Published by:

KP Publishing Company
Content Producers
of Fiction, Nonfiction & Children's Books
Valencia, CA 91355
www.kp-pub.com

Printed in the United States of America

PREFACE

As I sit outside of our home, in the backyard, adjacent to the park, I can't help but think about how far from "home" I have come. This world that I am so comfortable living in now was something I never knew existed. From the manicured lawns to the strip malls on every corner to the diverse population of people in my own community, I still can't believe that this is now my world and home and I'm so incredibly grateful for my life.

My name is Veronica Gandarilla-Bornn and I am a Mexicana. I was born and raised in a small Mexican town in the state of Guerrero, near the town of Arcelia, Tlapehuala and Altamirano (San Jose de Poliutla Gro, Mexico).

Our family lived here until I was 9 years old, at which time we immigrated to the United States. Once in America, my life would evolve and change into what it is today: daily thanking God for His blessings.

Author Veronica Bornn
(On the hill where the title was inspired)

DEDICATION

To all the loves of my life, those still with us and those who have passed. My husband Jason, my children Angelo, Julian, and Paloma, my dad, my beautiful mom, mother-in-law Susan Bornn, family, friends, and those who helped make this book possible. Last but not least, to my found love, Jesus Christ, my Lord, and my God.

CONTENTS

Preface — *v*
Dedication — *vii*
Forewords — *xi*
Introduction — *xvii*

CHAPTER 1	El Molino	1
CHAPTER 2	Leaving Poliutla	7
CHAPTER 3	Dad Promised to Come Back	13
CHAPTER 4	Meeting Dad in America	21
CHAPTER 5	El Barrio Pobre aka The Poor Town	27
CHAPTER 6	Pressured to Learn English and Grow Fast	33
CHAPTER 7	Going Back to Mexico	47
CHAPTER 8	My First Husband	57
CHAPTER 9	A Glimpse of Real Love	79
CHAPTER 10	I Found Love	97

Acknowledgment — *109*
About the Author — *111*
Afterword — *113*

FOREWORD

This book is the fruit of love's labor that is heartwarming and inspirational. It is a simple and honest portrayal of the author's journey, thus far. A challenging journey that draws the reader into Veronica's childhood and formative years growing up in Poliutla, Mexico. But through these challenges, she found the path that led to Jesus Christ.

As with any family, there are joys, disappointments, and trials! Veronica shares her daily life of growing up under the strong and loving influence of her mother. The author's mother chose to navigate her adversities with perseverance and integrity. Her mother's strength of character provided life-changing lessons that Veronica Bornn still applies, daily.

Steeped in her Mexican heritage lies her story. One in which respect and honor, especially towards elders, are significantly valued, and she has taught her children to do the same.

After a period of difficult circumstances, there is a beautiful and welcome development, through this journey of extreme adversities.

Veronica is a woman of strong faith. She loves God's Word and is passionate about living God's Word. She exemplifies that woman of faith and virtue in Proverbs 31.

Having known her for several years, I can unequivocally say that Veronica has consistently been an excellent example of what a wife and mother (apart from other roles!) she could be. She is a gentle, loving, and kind person who adores and respects her husband; and tenderly cares for her precious children, as well as her extended family. They, in turn, look up to her for godly wisdom and guidance.

Veronica is the epitome of the woman in Proverbs 31:8.

"Her children rise up, and call her blessed; her husband also, and he praiseth her."

To God be the glory.

Chandrika David, Santa Clarita, California
Author of *From Chandrika's Kitchen: Where Cooking is an Expression of Love*

FOREWORD

A friend of mine once said, "Life is a short bus ride through a rough neighborhood." I laughed. Then I teared up.

He's right. For as long as these days can be, the years are short. For as difficult as the seasons can seem, they do go quickly. And in the end, we are a sum of our choices and learnings from these experiences.

It's not odd to meet someone who has had a life that has taken many turns and encountered many difficulties.

My sister has lived one of those lives. At the age of 45, she has endured infertility, an abusive husband, a divorce, a second marriage to a gift from God, and then his untimely and shocking death. She's seen some things. She's felt some things. And these are the experiences that are making her who she is.

No, it's not odd to meet someone who has had difficulty, odds are you may be one as well. We all endure our share of twists and turns in the road; the question becomes, do we learn from them?

The city I live in has a street called Via Princessa. It stretches out all across the city. Judging by the fact that the name is evident on both sides of town, your assumption might be you could take it from one end of the city to another. But the locals will tell you, "they never connected it." There is a gap right in the middle. Trying to get across the valley on Via Princessa will take you "Via a dried-up riverbed."

The journey of our lives may seem similar, may seem troublesome, but the ones who truly succeed are the ones who examine their journey and listen to the locals. Sometimes roads need to be taken; sometimes, they need to be detoured. Sometimes, they never connected it.

The book you are about to read is an examined life that connects the dots of God's handiwork, Jesus' faithfulness, and a journey that even though it can be rough and short, it can lead to evidence of our heavenly Father's abundant blessing.

Rusty George, Lead Pastor,
Real Life Church, Santa Clarita, California
Author of *Better Together and After Amen!*

"Veronica Bornn takes us on a poignant, unfiltered journey of the highs and lows of her life. This is an emotional story that hooked me after chapter one. Veronica introduces us to her beautiful family and opens her heart as she tells stories of her life. She does this with wisdom from her mother and wisdom she has learned throughout the years. Veronica does eventually find love. Her journey is truly captivating. I appreciate the fact that she includes many battles that are not so rosy, with all the victories. ***I Found Love*** is incredibly well written. You won't want to put this book down. I highly recommend this book to my family and friends."

Tina Davis,
Technical Director, Fox Sports

INTRODUCTION

Teodomira

Not only was Teodomira my mom, beautiful and smart, but she was also strong, loving, and very hard-working. She loved to tend to her pet birds and even made a human-sized bird cage that held all kinds of colorful birds here in America.

Mom loved to garden and walk. On our walks, she would talk about life, her dreams, and her thoughts. We could walk and talk for days. On most of our middle-of-the-day walks,

Mom would drink a bottle of Pepsi, which she called "mi panzona" which means *my fatsie*.

Our walks together are what I keep with me today. Mom shared her life stories with me, and I want to pass a few of them onto you.

Teodomira, pronounced *tay-oh-doe-mida*, was a proud Mestiza. She was a woman of mixed race, having indigenous and Spanish descent. She was born and raised in Colonia, a little town in the state of Guerrero, Mexico, where everybody knew each other. She was the eldest of three children.

My grandmother left Mom when she was four years old in search of work in Mexico City, only to never return. Mom always wondered why her mom never came back, and the only explanation to her was that she must have died because she couldn't understand how a mother could leave her children behind.

My grandfather would eventually remarry a woman named Maria. Being a stepchild and the oldest, Mom was responsible for caring for her younger siblings. She had no childhood to enjoy as she cooked and cleaned. If Mom didn't do things according to Maria's expectations, she would be beaten.

One story Mom shared with me was when Maria threw a piece of broken pot at her, and it hit her on the head. It sliced a decent size gash on her head, bloodying up the ribbons in her hair.

Introduction

Maria then hid the bloody hair ribbons by burning them in the jogon, an outdoor firepit. Then she told Mom that if she said anything, she would take her to the mountains and leave her there to be eaten by the coyotes. Mom's reminder of this event was the memory of the scars on her head.

In Mexican culture, when a girl turns 15, it is customary for her parents to throw a quinceañera, a big celebration that centers around a young girl's transition from her childhood, to her recognition as an adult.

When Mom turned 15, Maria did not want to throw her the *quinceañera*.

It bothered my grandfather so much that he took Mom to the city and bought a beautiful, yet expensive rebozo, or shawl, as a gift.

The time that Mom and her father spent together was huge. And while this impressive gift made Mom feel special, the gesture upset Maria.

This act of kindness caused Maria to do a bad and an unthinkable thing.

Let me explain. In my culture, an unmarried woman who engages in premarital sex is considered impure and thus, much more difficult to find a husband for marriage.

Maria invited her brother over and while he was in the house, she left them alone and locked all the doors with the intent of encouraging her brother to rape Mom.

Mom fought him off and somehow managed to get out of the locked house, ran to her aunt's house, and explained what happened.

When Mom's aunt told Grandfather what had happened, he gave the young man, his brother-in-law, a severe beating.

Mom didn't tell Grandfather it was Maria who locked them in for fear of something far greater happening to her, if that was even possible.

My grandfather and Maria would chaperone Mom when she went to local dances as a *señorita*. A senorita is a young unmarried woman, old enough to be considered for marriage, but very carefully chaperoned to make sure that no man could have a chance to take advantage of her youth and inexperience.

The resourceful nature of Mom was on display. When she needed money for the dances, she would ask Grandfather if she could sell the leftover fruit from the mango trees. With that money, she would get her hair done and buy dresses to wear to the local dances.

It was at one of those dances where she met her first love, Humberto. He came from a good family and was an only child. Soon his family and a priest made arrangements to talk to Grandfather about marriage.

The possibility of her personal maid, Mom, being married did not make Maria happy, and it became evident she wasn't going to let Mom go without a fight. It became her mission to stop the marriage.

Introduction

First, she told Grandfather that Mom's boyfriend only wanted to marry her because he thought they were rich. Grandfather owned a great deal of farmland, with animals, and mango trees. He didn't believe Maria because he had spoken with his future son-in-law and it was clear that Humberto loved Mom.

Since Maria couldn't convince Grandfather, she went directly to Mom's future in-laws. Maria told them that she could swear to them on a Bible that my mother was not a virgin, and their son should not marry her.

In Mexico, it is customary for a young lady to be a virgin and wear a white dress on her wedding day. Since our town is small and everyone knows each other, it is likely that a non-virgin girl would bring shame to the potential groom's family. Mom's future in-laws believed Maria's words and the marriage was canceled. Mom was heartbroken and didn't understand why they didn't have the decency to give her an explanation.

While out shopping one day, Mom saw Humberto and smiled. He stopped to talk to her. She swallowed hard and listened to him profess his love and hoped to ask her to marry him again. But it was too late. Mom couldn't forgive him for allowing the false allegations to stop the marriage plans.

Mom went on with her life and eventually would meet and marry our father, Camilo, whose nickname was Cuerno, which means Horn. He would often come to Colonia for the dances they held and after meeting Mom, he came to see Mom more regularly.

In our culture, there are only two ways a woman gets married. One, is that both sets of parents of the prospective couple agree to the marriage, and it happens or the other, is the boy sneaks over to the girl's house at night, "kidnaps" her, with her permission, and takes her to his home.

It is a predetermined event by the couple, and they are fully aware of what they are doing and what the consequence will be. In most cases, the boy's parents and family are aware of the event and are willing to participate. It does not mean that the couple engages in premarital sex, but it does mean that marriage is the intended outcome. The next morning, the apologetic bridegroom's parents visit the bride-to-be's home and present reconciliation gifts as they would assure arrangements for the union.

During Mom's generation, this seemingly archaic method of kidnapping was a frequent and customary routine. In some cases, the boy's parents did not know he was going to do this. In these instances, the young couple thought they were ready and would carry out the plan on their own. In other cases, the parents of either the boy or girl (or both sets of parents) did not approve of their children's selection or thought they were too young, or they didn't approve of the partner. Regardless of the reason, this practice happened often.

Introduction

In Mom's case, she saw it as an escape from her home. She loved my dad and wanted to marry him and was not about to take any chances of Maria sabotaging it. So, with that, she agreed to leave her home and go with him.

As was the custom of that time, on the day of the "kidnapping," the bride-to-be remained at the bridegroom's parents house until their wedding day. As I previously mentioned, the only way a girl can wear a white wedding dress on her wedding day is for her to be a virgin.

The only people who can determine if the girl is a virgin are the parents of the groom. They determine this by their observation and feeling about the couple and whether or not they feel that they have in fact been abstaining from sex. If there is any doubt on their part, it was not uncommon for the parents to bring the girl to a doctor to have her examined and determine if she was a virgin or not.

In Mom's case, she was married in a white dress that was specially made for her and purchased by Dad's mother in Mexico City.

The last time Mom saw her first love, Humberto, she was happily married with three children. She sat next to my grandfather at my Aunt Ramina's wedding. She noticed his familiar frame and face as he danced before her. Seeing him again did nothing for Mom as he was dancing. But he did request their song be played, "Tu Enamorado" by Pedro Infante, before she left.

Maybe he thought this would spark some sort of interest in Mom that would encourage her to have a conversation with him, or maybe it was his way of saying sorry and gaining closure, or maybe he just felt sentimental. But Mom had already made it very clear that she was not going to talk to him and whatever efforts he made by dancing in front of her or playing their old song would fall on deaf ears. Mom had already moved on.

CHAPTER 1

EL MOLINO

One morning, in our town of Poliutla, Mom was standing in line to get her corn ground into *masa* (dough used to make tortillas). Typically, each family in the town would grow their own food, mainly corn, which was harvested, cooked, dried out, and then brought to "El Molino" (the store that had a machine to grind the corn into masa).

While in line, she overheard several women talking about some young boys who had broken into one of the local stores through the roof and stole some beer. The town was full of these street front stores, which were simply the front half of people's homes. According to these women, the owner of the store knew who had broken in and was going to leave the opening in the roof unlocked so that the thieves, who would inevitably return for more would enter and meet their untimely deaths at the end of the owner's shotgun. The owner would be justified of course, as the intruders would have been guilty of trespassing.

It just so happened that my brother, Pablo, had gotten himself involved with this shady group of boys. He was lured by the owner's son to go through the roof and steal beer. These so-called *friends* seemed to never have had my brother's best interests in mind and I was always curious as to why he felt a connection to them.

I always felt like Pablo was a stud who was really good at everything he did. When it came to spear fishing, he always came home with fish. If he was playing soccer, he was always the first pick. When running races, he rarely lost. Anyone who challenged him to a fist fight learned quickly that he was a formidable opponent. If he was riding a bull, he was great at it. Sometimes he was doing some of these things behind Mom's back.

I know this because I saw firsthand the parade, dancing, and bull-riding when Grandpa Francisco would take me to our town's festivities that fell in October. On this particular day, my brother chose the biggest, toughest, and scariest bull to ride because no one else would ride it. Some bull riders and even the best-experienced ones wouldn't sign up to ride it. But guess what? My brother Pablo did.

I was on top of my grandpa's shoulders and I could see it all. My brother rode on that bull for a long time until the bull reared its head back and pierced my brother's throat with one of its pointy horns. I saw blood gush out from his throat, and I screamed and cried as he was carried into a *camioneta*, or minivan, to Arcelia for medical attention. This time, I thought my brother was close to losing his life.

Another story I remember about my brother was when he went fishing with one of his friends. That day, Mom started to worry because it was getting dark and Pablo hadn't returned yet. Earlier that day, Pablo left with a clean, white tee shirt and now it was blood-stained and filthy. I remember my brother not looking like he was well. Mom peeled the blood-soaked shirt from his body and saw his wounds. Pablo had been stabbed with a spear fishing rod multiple times by a so-called *friend*.

Other stories I heard were about friends challenging him to fistfights, and every time he would end up on top with the win. It didn't matter if he was playing a sport, running in a foot race, or throwing rocks, he was great at it. Pablo was an alpha male. Because of how good he was at everything and the jealousy that seeped from so-called friends, who would trick him, go behind his back, and act cowardly. No wonder Mom took what she heard so seriously.

Initially, Mom thought it was just the curious nature of a boy that was leading him into some bad choices and decisions. But this time, his choices had led him to the possibility of his death at the hands of the storeowner.

It was at this point that Mom had to do what she felt she needed to do to protect and save her son. Mom was in fear that he would get in more trouble with his friends.

Mom would do anything to protect us and be our voice and strength. I saw the struggle to just live. But she made it a happy, loving adventure for us.

If we were poor, we didn't know it, because we had all that we thought we needed. Mom took pride in what she had and ensured that we were always well washed, groomed, and dressed. We were very blessed to have a mother that cared and didn't allow the fact that we didn't have a lot of money stop her from doing that for us.

Based on our appearance, other kids in the town thought we had money, but that wasn't the case. We had enough to eat and live, that's it. I remember when the school had materials to give out for free, we were never the lucky ones because according to them we didn't need them because we could afford it and we were rich.

Another thing I remember was that Mom had to go through so much work just to get a tortilla on the table and that's what I mean when I say she was a hard-working woman. I got to see how it was not having all the luxuries that I have today (refrigerator, dishwasher, washer/dryer, microwave, indoor plumbing, etc.) and yet, she found pleasure in doing the things that needed to be done with love and pride.

Some days were harder than others like the days she had to go wash clothes at the river. Near our town was "El Rio" (The River) in which the people of my town washed their clothes. This would entail carrying all the dirty clothes in a basket (Mom would carry it on her head) for about a mile to the river. Once there, she would find a spot where to begin the process of hand washing the clothes. Mom would find a big flat rock near the water's edge, dip the clothes in, pour soap on the clothing, and begin the strenuous process of rolling the

El Molino

material against itself and the rock. Once she was done scrubbing the clothing, Mom would dip it back into the river to rinse the soap off and lay the clothing out on rocks, bushes, or trees to dry off in the sun.

This was an exceedingly difficult process in that it involved multiple repetitions of grinding and rolling the cloth with the soap. It was no wonder that Mom's grip was so strong.

Also just making a meal was a big production. It would start with starting the fire in the "*jogon.*" The *jogon* was a clay stove that was fat on the bottom and with an opening at the top. It had an opening on the side where branches, wood would be placed, lit on fire, and the heat would rise through an opening on the top.

A "*comal*" (a flat pan made of clay) would be placed over the opening on top of the jogon, which would serve as the heating surface for the tortillas, pots, and pans.

Sometimes just getting the fire started would be the biggest challenge. Luckily, Mom had my older brothers Dario, Pablo and Alejandro to help her. Dario would take the corn to the Molino to be ground into dough, while Pablo and Alejandro would gather up branches and wood for the fire.

My older sister Coco, baby sister Carina, and I would be busy playing among the many mango trees we had in our yard.

These are just some of the things that Mom went through daily. My father, who at this point was living in America, was not there to help. Mom was on her own with the six of us and each day brought on a new set of challenges. But with each of these challenges, she pressed on and made it look easy.

Mom believed in her dreams and told me to believe in mine too. She left those qualities to me and I'm so grateful for them. Maybe to some people's standards her dreams were tiny, but for her they were huge. I saw all her dreams come to life. Some of her dreams were to give us a better life by coming to America, owning her own house and car, and giving us a better life. A good life to her was waking up, loving every minute of the day, and doing things that mattered to her.

Mom loved doing things for us, whether it was making flower vases for each of us, cooking our favorite meals, or taking us on one of her epic walks that she was notorious for taking. Regardless of the activity, Mom accepted that each day was a blessing and made the most of it. She instilled that in us and made sure that we never forgot where we came from, and what we could become. She was living a life with passion and enjoyment no matter the circumstances. This was one of the many gifts Mom passed on to us.

CHAPTER 2

LEAVING POLIUTLA

One morning when it was still dark out, we left our home in Mexico forever. Mom's sense of protection was the primary reason we left Mexico for the United States of America. It was hard for us, for her, to leave the only place we, she, had ever known. For her to leave it behind took a tremendous leap of faith.

At the time she decided to leave our small town for the United States of America, she had six children. Dario, who was the oldest and going to school, living with my uncle in Mexico City. Between Pablo, Alejandro, Coco, myself, and Carina, this left a tough choice for Mom as to who else would not make the trip to America.

When Mom decided to leave Mexico for Pablo's protection, she could not afford to take all five of us. Pablo was in danger of being seriously injured or even killed by not only the store owner, but also by other young men in our small town who were jealous of him for being a good athlete and a good fighter, too. The choice was going to be difficult mainly due to the amount of kids Mom had to take.

Even though Mom said this would be temporary, I know it was breaking her heart, having to choose who would stay and who would go. She felt it was risky leaving a girl behind. In the end, it was Alejandro who would be left behind with my grandma. He was a good son who avoided trouble. Mom hoped that she could get enough money to send for him soon.

That night she convinced Pablo to stay home instead of letting him hang out with his friends in fear of him getting into more trouble before we left. She didn't tell anyone what her plans were.

God provided the right time, because that day my cousin, Emi, was supposed to leave our town to go back to the United States of America. Her mom Camila had sent her on vacation to visit my grandma, and this was the night she was also leaving the town.

It was still dark when Mom woke us up, dressed, and hurried us off to the bus stop on the main road that went through our town. Emi was already waiting there. Once the bus arrived, Mom took a seat for two people, even though there was five of us.

My cousin had her own seat and sat next to Pablo. Mom told Coco and I to get under the seats and to not make any noise while she held Carina in her arms and sat next to Pablo. We didn't completely understand why, but we did exactly as she said.

Leaving Poliutla

The next thing I remember was arriving in Tijuana. As I grew older and wiser, I figured out why Mom smuggled us onto the bus—because she didn't have enough money. She would do anything to make sure she didn't leave us behind. I know that she would even beg if she had to in order for us to come with her.

Veronica in the middle

My father, who was living and working in America, would visit us in the town every couple of years and return back to the U.S. My memories of his visits are vague, but the fact that Mom kept having children nine months after he left was proof of his coming and going.

Mom's plan was to arrive in Tijuana and call my dad to come pick us up. She didn't bother calling and letting him know ahead of time because she wasn't sure if he would have supported her decision. This way, with us so close to him on the border, he would not have a choice but to come get us.

When we arrived at the bus depot that evening in Tijuana, my cousin, who was a U.S. citizen and could legally travel to the U.S. was picked up by her mom, my Dad's sister, Camila. We waited for our Dad to pick us up.

We searched and found an affordable motel for the night. Next to the hotel entrance, there was a small liquor store that Mom took us into to buy some soda and chips. I picked out a bag of something I had never seen before and decided to give it a try—Cheetos.

When I opened the bag, the smell was very intriguing. That lasted only until I tasted them. I was not used to the processed flavor and the cheesy taste made me nauseous. Coco had selected Doritos, but they weren't much better. Our long trip had removed us from our town and brought us one step closer to the United States of America.

Once Mom checked us in, she left the room, went to a payphone, called Dad, and told him that we were in Tijuana and that he needed to come get us. I remember climbing into the bed with Mom that night. I still remember resting on

Mom's body and her arms around me. The bed was against the wall. The lights went off.

I also remember sobbing, because I was sad that we had left our home in Mexico. Mom heard and asked if I was okay, but I pretended to be asleep and didn't answer. I was sad about having to leave home, but I knew as long as Mom was with us, we were safe, and we would be ok.

CHAPTER 3

DAD PROMISED TO COME BACK

As long as I can remember, Dad was rarely with us in Mexico. He had made the decision that in order for him to financially support his growing family, he needed to travel to the U.S. to find work and send the money back to us in Mexico. He would visit us a few times a year but it seemed with each passing year, the visits became less frequent and his stays in the U.S. would last longer. When Dad visited us in Mexico, it always seemed like it was for a few days at a time. I don't remember much, but what I do remember was that his sister, Camila, had arrived from the United States, too, and the two of them were always together, busy visiting the town and going dancing and partying. It bothered me. I'm sure it bothered Mom, too.

One particular time, when it was time for Dad to leave, and we had hardly seen him, I remember asking him to stay as I tearfully held onto him.

Dad said he could make more money working in the United States than in Mexico, but as a five-year old, I couldn't understand his need to abandon us for work. I understand now that this was a way for him to be responsible and caring for his growing family. I clung to him ever so tightly. The hot tears rushed down my face like a waterfall as he promised me, he would come back. He pulled away from me, said he loved me, and got onto the bus.

I sobbed as I stood there watching the bus drive away, getting smaller and smaller. For however many years it was after that, I wrote him daily as I expressed how much I loved and missed him. I would ask him for things to bring back to us the next time he came back to see us.

In the meantime, Mom would get busy tending to us, her

cows, mango trees, guava trees, papaya trees and flowers. She would sell flowers, mangos, and mango trees to the high school kids for their agricultural class.

Mom even sold cow's milk, cheese, and just about anything to bring money in. The rest was for us to enjoy and eat. We would keep ourselves busy with school and playing. We would also help by running errands for her. Sometimes, Mom sent us to my Uncle Samuel's market to get things we needed. He took note of the list and helped us get them.

Other times, like when money was low, Mom sent us to Grandma's house to get things like chilies or tomatoes or just about anything else we didn't have. Despite money being tight, she managed to come up with money to pay the credit bills.

Dad, meanwhile, working in the United States, would send money to us. Grandma got it first and determined the amount to give to my mother. I don't know why they did it that way, but I know I didn't like it. It was like Mom was being treated like a child and didn't know how to spend the money on things that we needed.

Mom made sure she didn't sit around waiting for Dad's money and would find creative ways to make sure we didn't go without our basic needs.

Our house was small, but our land was a good size. We had about thirty-eight grown mango trees and each one of us had our own mango tree that Mom designated for us. We also had four guava trees, one on each corner of the land, two papaya trees in the middle of the property, and a garden of exotic beautiful flowers.

I remember every day after school we would run up onto our mango trees and count how many mangos we had. We would wait patiently until those mangos were ready to eat. But there were those times when our mangos would disappear, and we didn't know what happened to them. I would ask my brothers and sisters but apparently theirs were missing, too. Then one day, the mystery of the disappearing mangos was solved. We saw a pig digging in the dirt. When we walked up on the pig, we found a buried suitcase, that belonged to Coco, filled with mangos. No wonder she left me behind going to school. She would take the ripe mangos and sell them to kids at school. I saw them run to Coco and pay her their money. Now, I know why she could always buy me my favorite *saladitas*—salty crackers-without a fight.

The mango trees were a prominent topic of conversation between Grandpa and Mom. He would try to discourage her from planting them. He would say, "Teodomira, why do you bother planting those tiny trees? Do you know you're not even going to have the chance to taste those mangos? It will take forever for them to grow and someone other than you are going to enjoy them."

Mom would always say, "It's okay if I don't get to see the fruit of my labor because my kids will." And as usual, Mom was right. Those mango trees grew, gave fruit, and we all ate them and even Grandpa did too.

Mom often spoke of how people would attempt to discourage her from accomplishing her goals, but those attempts were for naught. She believed hard work always paid off. I have such a tender heart for my mom. I know how exhausted she was and despite that, she loved to make the days special and wanted our days to be filled with tender, loving care.

I remember on long hot nights Mom would put our mattresses under the mango trees. We stared at the moon and bright stars as she sang and told stories.

"Que habia un gato con sus pies de trapo y sus hojos alrevez, quires Que te lo cuente otra vez?" She was saying there once was a cat with cloth paws and his eyes were backwards. The end.

Do you want me to tell you the story again?" she asked. We yelled yes, and even if she was tired, she never showed it, as we would ask for more stories, like *"Uncle Donkey and The Caiman"* and songs.

We watched the stars and listened to her as she never denied us even as we drifted off to sleep soon after. Mom worked hard and was often tired. But no matter how weary she would be, she would always tell us our favorite stories.

This was her way of making us stop asking for more and making us go to sleep so we would just stare at the moon and the stars and eventually fall asleep.

One of my most favorite stories was *The Story of Uncle Donkey* and *The Caiman*. There was once a donkey that was taking a stroll when he heard a voice ask for help, "Uncle Donkey, Uncle Donkey help me." The voice came from a Caiman.

Uncle Donkey asked him, "How can I help you?"

The Caiman responded, "I need you to take me to the ocean because my lake dried out and I will die if I don't make it to the ocean."

Uncle Donkey thought about it and said, "If I take you to the ocean, I'm afraid you might bite me and eat me."

The Caiman assured Uncle Donkey that would not be the case and promised he wouldn't. The Caiman said, "Uncle Donkey by taking me to the ocean, you are saving my life, so how could I turn around and eat you?"

In the end, the Caiman convinced Uncle Donkey. Once at the ocean the Caiman kept asking uncle Donkey to take him a little more into the ocean, a little more ended up being deep in the water, suddenly the Caiman was about to bite Uncle Donkey. Uncle Donkey couldn't believe it!

Poor Uncle Donkey asked the Caiman, "How can you do this to me when you promised me that you would not eat me?" The Caiman's response was, "Oh Uncle Donkey, don't you know that good is always re-paid with bad?" Uncle Donkey said, "That's not true!" and started crying.

The Caiman then said, "Listen so that you can see I'm fair. I'm going to ask the first three living souls I see pass by the following question: 'Isn't it true that good is re-paid with bad?' If just one of them answers 'NO!' then you are free to leave."

Aunt Paloma was flying by so the Caiman asked, "Aunt Paloma isn't it true that good is always re-paid with bad?", and she responded, "Aaaaaaaaaaaaaalways."

Then Aunt Turtle passed by and the Caiman asked, "Isn't it true Aunt Turtle that a good is always re-paid with a bad?," and she answered, "Aaaaaaaaaaaaalways."

Finally, Uncle Rabbit passed by and the Caiman asked, "Isn't it true Uncle Rabbit that a good is always re-paid with a bad?"

Now Uncle Rabbit, being very intelligent before answering, wanted to get to the bottom of what was going on. So he said, "What, I can't hear you come a little closer?" The Caiman got a little closer and repeated the question but Uncle Rabbit kept saying, "What? I can't hear you, come a little closer," and so it continued until the Caiman was close to the sand.

They were so close that Uncle Rabbit could whisper to Uncle Donkey, "Why don't you just jump?" Uncle Donkey being a donkey couldn't understand.

The Caiman finally yelled at the top of his lungs, "Isn't it true Uncle Rabbit a good is always repaid with a bad?" Uncle

Rabbit whispered more urgently to Uncle Donkey who finally understood, jumped and escaped.

Then Uncle Rabbit finally answered the Caiman, "ALL OF THE TIME!" as he hopped away.

These stories were some of my fondest memories while in Mexico with Mom while my Dad was away. I would have rather had him there with us in our home, but given the circumstances, it was the best we could do.

CHAPTER 4

MEETING DAD IN AMERICA

The next day in Tijuana, Mom explained to us what the plan was for us to get into America. Mom would get in on her own with Pablo and my baby sister, Carina, while my sister Coco and I would be picked up by my Dad's friend, Hector. The night time was an easier time to cross the border.

On the day we were picked up, we were wearing our *pastora* green dresses. We wore these dresses during the Christmas season with groups of kids in our small town as we sang *pastorelas*—Christmas carolling, so to speak.

When Hector arrived, I noticed right away how tall he was and that he had a pot belly. He was dark skinned, had a fresh haircut, and was wearing a baby blue guayabera shirt and jeans. He arrived in a shiny green Chevy Impala that looked new to me.

Hector's wife was with him to pose as our mother so that we did not have any issues with the border patrol. She had wavy short black hair and was wearing a white blouse and beige slacks. As we climbed into the car, I could not help but notice how clean the car was. I sat behind Hector while my sister sat behind his wife.

Before we arrived at the border check point, he coached us on what to do. We were to pretend to be asleep so that the agents would leave us alone, but he prepared us for what to say just in case they woke us up. Sure enough, when we got to the check point, the border patrol agent woke us up and on cue, we told the agent our names, ages, and that we were the daughters of Hector.

With that, we crossed the border into America. I did not understand why our Dad could not pick us up on his own until later.

I remember thinking how pretty this place was. It was bright with many lights and I thought, *How fun it must be to live here.* I was taken aback by all the colorful California freeway signs, billboards, and advertisements. I remember attempting to read each one as we drove along the highway until I fell asleep.

We finally stopped at my Aunt Camila's one-bedroom apartment. These one-bedroom apartments were like little individual houses but all connected together in a rectangular format. In the middle of the apartments was dirt with plants. This apartment was even smaller now that there were five other people there. I kept thinking there was no way anyone else could fit. I was wrong.

Meeting Dad in America

A few days later, Mom, Carina, and Pablo arrived. It wasn't much longer after that, Dad looked for a bigger place for us to live in. During the time at my aunt's we met the family that lived in one of the corner apartments.

I remember Coco and I mostly played with Nina and Mona. Nina was older so she would sometimes take us to the liquor store nearby. I remember Nina's favorite snack to get which was peeled sunflower salty seeds. My favorite candy to get was *Now or Later* or the *Ring Pop* because I got more for my money (only five cents for an 8 pack of *Now or Later* or *Ring Pop*).

Sometimes I would splurge and spend ten cents on one of my other favorite treats which was mini chocolate balls in a pack of ten. The candy would last while we freely played around the complex.

While Dad looked for adequate housing Mom enrolled us into the local elementary school. It was about six blocks away from my Aunt Camila's apartment. The first day of school was interesting to say the least. As new immigrants to America, we entered our classrooms speaking zero English.

I sat next to a very nice girl that tried to translate what the teacher was saying but it was little help to me. I looked at the blackboard with a blank stare on my face, lost and confused, as the teacher taught and walked back and forth. I wrote the notes from the chalk board in my notebook, but they made no sense.

We were given specific instructions by Mom as to what to do at the end of the school day. She said, "Get your sister Carina and meet me in front of the school." Coco and I got to the front of the school where Carina's classroom was but didn't see her. We went and searched the restrooms, by the playground, cafeteria, in other classrooms, and the office. Where could she be? We left school and went down many unfamiliar streets as we screamed her name in painful and unsuccessful vain. Coco and I would say to each other, "What if she is being hurt inside that house?"

The sun was setting, and the panic was rising within us as it was becoming clearer that we were not close to finding Carina. We knew Mom was going to be upset with us. To make matters worse, we were now lost, wandering aimlessly. We happened onto a woman who was watering her lawn. Unfortunately, she didn't speak Spanish, so we feverishly resorted to sign language in hopes of getting her to understand the gravity of our situation.

She pointed us into an unfamiliar direction and lo and behold, a car with teenagers we recognized from our apartment complex were driving by. They recognized us and got us in the car and ended up bringing us home to our parents.

Dad and Mom were outside and they looked stressed. The car door opened and Mom's face was one of relief when she finally saw us. Coco and I would find out that our younger sister Carina had been picked up by one of our older cousins,

Beto, who was also picking up his baby sister, who was in the same classroom as Carina and had brought her home. He thought he was doing us a favor, but in the end, it caused a lot of stress for everyone.

That night, I went to sleep feeling safe and complete knowing that part of my family was together here in America. But I couldn't help thinking about my town, Poliutla. Each night, I would walk the streets of my town in my mind and as I laid there in bed, I would say the names of the people living in each home. I did this so I wouldn't forget where I came from and, in the event that we did return home, I would remember everyone.

I made it through everyday always remembering were I came from and hoping to go back one day, and I would pray that our mango trees would be watered. I was complete and always had the most comforting feeling when sleeping next to Mom.

CHAPTER 5

EL BARRIO POBRE AKA THE POOR TOWN

We moved out from my aunt's cramped, one-bedroom apartment and were able to stay with Mom's cousin in their apartment in Long Beach, California, for a few days before getting into our new apartment. It was called El Barrio Pobre—*the Poor Town*. It was a large complex filled with small apartments.

The people that lived there were mostly people that came here from Mexico. They came here to earn money to send back home to their families. These small, yet affordable living spaces, provided a roof and bed for them. Some families were just making enough money to pay rent, send money back home, and whatever was left was for food and bills. They worked hard, were content and seemed happy. To them, this lifestyle served as an opportunity to support and better their family's future.

America was the place that inspired dreams to come true, with hard work and belief. I remember that small apartment had a tiny 5x7 TV in it. We didn't think anything of it because we were content with the little we had, and all that ever mattered to us, was that we were loved and safe. We never cared much for material things. It didn't mean we didn't want anything, but what we needed was provided by Mom which was love and safety because the truth was, Dad was working hard to provide for us. Now looking back, I can see the sacrifices made by him, too. He had a lot of responsibilities heaped on his shoulders and he was trying hard to keep up.

Soon after we moved into our new Long Beach apartment on Almond and 10th Street. There was a buzz to the apartment complex we moved into. The building had four apartments and there were three families, the Flores', the Arrajo's, and the Garzas', living in the three other apartments.

El Barrio Pobre aka The Poor Town

The nice thing was that the Arrajo's and Garzas' families came from the same town as us in Mexico.

What fun it was to actually know people in America. We would become good friends with these families. The girls who lived in the complex, Dory, Flora, Annie, and us would spend a lot of time with each other.

Sometimes we would fight and not always get along, but when we did, we would gather all the neighbor kids and play school or beauty salon and would hold pageants. We would make up shows or set competitions on best hairdos. We sure found many ways to keep busy and entertained.

Soon after we were enrolled into a new school, Lincoln Elementary. I was assigned to my new teacher. Mrs. Robinson, who intimidated me. She wasn't mean to me, but it was because I had never seen a tall, black woman in my life.

I thought she was an Amazon woman from the comics I read in Mexico. Then again, I was missing Coco. Ever since I could remember, we were always in the same class. I begged Mom to put us in the same class and she did.

I was transferred to Coco's class, taught by Ms. Harper, who was tall and thin with long blond hair. She often wore a starched-ironed shirt and tan loose-fitting pants. I was pleased to be in the same class as Coco, since we had always been together in every class since we were small.

When we were at school, Coco sat in front of a funny boy

named Jesus. He was very distracting. He would tap her on the shoulder as he giggled. I could see him giggling all the time. I really think Jesus liked Coco, but she didn't pay much attention to him.

Ms. Harper was a very nice person. You could tell she genuinely cared about all her students. She would allow all her students to check out books from her classroom shelf. Coco was the one who would check out the most and when we got home, we looked at the pictures and tried to read the words. I learned to read a little bit more, not perfectly, but I could understand a little.

When we would get home from school, I was expected to read the mail for Mom. Since I understood more English than my siblings and Mom did not speak any English, the responsibility of reading the mail fell on me which was something I did not enjoy.

As soon as we were settled into our new apartment. Mom was aware that she still had two kids in Mexico and she kept saving her money to bring my brothers home. Soon she had enough money to send for Dario and Alejandro. This was a big deal to her, and it was her first priority. Once they were with us, she enrolled them into Franklin Jr. High and Millikan High School.

I watched and learned, at an early age, to keep my priorities in order. I learned to work hard and not be dissuaded by other people's words or judgements. I knew if I stayed focused, trusted my own values, everything would work out for me and my family.

Mom worked hard to give us a healthy happy life and it didn't cost her much but her unconditional love and patience. She wanted a better future for us so we didn't have to struggle like her.

She would always encourage us to read after school. I didn't always understand every word in these English books. But Mom insisted that I read anyway, because she believed by doing so, I would learn English faster.

I remember I was just starting to learn how to count in English and I was very excited I could count to the number 16. I kept repeating my numbers over and over so that I wouldn't forget. I was feeling very proud.

One particular night stands out because I was lying next to Dad getting ready to fall asleep. Even now, this beautiful memory will be cherished forever, because it is one of the best memories, I have of me and Dad. It gave me the satisfaction of knowing he loved us, even if it wasn't perfect, it was love.

He told me to count for him and explained to me that after sixteen all I have to do is change the ending and continue counting like in the beginning from 1-10 that the only difference was to add "teen" to the number seven at the end and go on to seventeen, eighteen, nineteen and taught me "twenty" and said to start all over but now change the beginning (twenty one twenty two and that night I discovered that I could count to forever if I only worked on the transition of every set of numbers.

I was so excited I couldn't stop counting and couldn't go to sleep. That night I went to sleep counting. Dad took the time to teach me and I really enjoyed and appreciated that so much, because he was the first person to have the patience to teach me. My teachers never stopped to help me in that way, or even knew about my needs in learning. I wanted to learn and was excited to learn but didn't know how. Learning was difficult, primarily due to the fact that I was in the wrong grade. They had me in the 6th grade when I should have been in the 4th grade.

CHAPTER 6

PRESSURED TO LEARN ENGLISH AND GROW FAST

In Mexico, all you need is a little bit of money and you can *buy* yourself a birth certificate with a *desired* birth date. Mom wanted me and my sister to be in the same classroom. Back in Mexico, I pressed Mom, even in tears, to let me go to school with my sister every day until I finally exhausted her. It paid off because she bought me a birth certificate.

With my *special* piece of paper in hand, I was ready to go to school with Coco. Our experience together began in the first grade. We had Señora. Lucrecia, who I distinctly remember having a paddle. That paddle was used for when we misbehaved. Let me tell you, I experienced it more than once.

For Coco, I was a pest to be around and that frustrated my sister. She didn't like the fact that I was in her class and that she was in some way responsible for me. Coco didn't always want to go to school and she would skip school to go find those kids that didn't attend school. Then, she would play marbles with them all day long, and I would just have to deal with it and wait. She was kind of a tomboy, and would play with boys all the time. She was so good at playing the marble game. She would beat them and take most of their marbles. She would then find an empty Coke glass bottle and fill it up with all her new colorful marbles.

When we finally made it to school, I would sometimes fall asleep in class and the teacher would just let me sleep. I guess one less kid to have to teach was not a bad idea. My teacher probably knew I wasn't the age Mom was saying I was, and she figured she was doing Mom a favor by keeping me in her class, so she didn't mind if I slept or not. Now that I think about it, I should have been home napping, because I was still little and probably needed my naps.

Now that we were in the United States, I ended up in Coco's grade because of the *purchased* Mexican birth certificate. We are not identical, or fraternal twins and we certainly didn't look alike. I was a 9-year-old that would be turning 10 the summer of my 6th grade year. Mom didn't see anything wrong with that, because I managed to stay on top of things, and always blended in with the rest of the kids. Teachers might have thought I was small for my age but all they needed was a birth certificate, real or otherwise, and in my case, it didn't matter. Plus, I acted mature for my age even though I was younger and I was more social than Coco.

Pressured to Learn English and Grow Fast

In America I had a harder time, because I wasn't just trying to act and be older, but I was trying to learn English, and on top of all that I was missing school too, because Mom became pregnant soon after. She had to have her required doctor's appointments and always needed someone to translate for her. That someone was me and she counted on me to go with her.

I felt the pressure to be grown up, to learn fast, and to be an even greater help to Mom especially now given her current state. I know it wasn't Mom's intension to do that to me, but she had no other choice at the time. Besides doing my homework every day, I was also reading the mail that came home.

After starting junior high school, I was quickly placed into regular English classes. My ESL (English as a second language) teacher felt I was ready. I disagreed. Although, it was hard, I still managed to pass my classes.

My favorite subjects were typing and art. To me, they seemed to be the easiest and didn't require much thought. All I had to do was look at the letters and type what was in front of me. Art was the same, I would just draw what was in front of me. I felt that I was placed in regular classes too soon and felt like I wasn't quite getting it and always felt behind even though my teacher didn't think so. I didn't feel like I knew where to go to get help and felt that I just had to do it all on my own.

It wasn't long after that we welcomed the newest addition—Adan—to our growing family. The after school routine changed to where now, after homework, we watched Adan while Mom prepared dinner for us and Dad's lunch for the next day. Once she was done with that, we would go out and play with the neighbor kids almost every day until Dad arrived home from work just in time for dinner.

Tuesday was a fun day as our parents would always buy us a treat from the produce truck that came every Tuesday evening to sell fresh produce and other things.

Sometimes, if we didn't have money, they kept a tab so that the next time around when we had it, my parents would pay them back.

Weekends were for soccer and family time. On most Saturdays, there was a party or gathering during the late afternoon and early evening at someone from our hometown's house. When there was no gathering, I remember Dad driving us in his bluish truck to the movies to see the latest Bruce Lee movie. If we weren't going to the movies then we were watching some old Bruce Lee movies or Spanish Western movies at home as a family.

On Sundays, every man, woman, and child met up at El Dorado Park for soccer games. We grew up Catholic, but we never really went to Church. Our fancy Bible with pictures sat on the coffee table as decoration, but I never remember really reading it. I recall only going to church during weddings, and Quinceañeras. I also remember thinking that I couldn't reach God and that the only way to reach him was going through someone else (the Priest, confess, be forgiven, then pray and God will hear my prayers). I also remember thinking "I was cheating by praying without confessing my sins."

At the park most of the kids did more playing than watching the adults play soccer. The highlight of these days was always getting ice cream from the ice cream truck. When we gathered at someone's home on Saturday evenings, often times there was music and dancing involved. As we were getting older, more and more, it seemed that men would ask us to dance.

Mom explained that it was rude to reject their dance advances. She said, "You aren't marrying them." She expressed to us to be humble and no matter how they look, respect them.

So, we did. It doesn't matter what you look like on the outside, you can be just as beautiful on the inside, and that's the pure spirit of love we get from God. Mom was adamant about us girls not marrying from our hometown in Mexico. She wanted us "cast a wide net" for our future husbands. She impressed on us to get a better life. Mom did her best to give us the advice we needed as young girls.

We loved and respected everything Mom had to say. I know I was a good daughter and all I wanted was to make her proud. I believed in my heart that if I obeyed Mom, that for sure God would bless me with a great future. The few times we went to church, I recalled a verse from the Bible saying children should "honor and obey their parents" or something like that. I knew I feared doing the wrong thing and ending up paying the consequences of my bad choices. I felt safe that if I did everything the right way and obeyed my parents that I would be okay.

Mom always took the time to talk to us. I really enjoyed listening to what she had to say, and I trusted her. I could tell her anything and I always knew how much she cared and loved me and that she would not judge me at all.

Sometimes Mom would get upset when Dad would bring his friends and drinking buddy—Aunt Camila—over. Most of the time if he wanted to decompress, he would go out and play cards with Aunt Camila and friends he usually went to his buddies' houses. Mom did not like him bringing them to our home, because she was concerned about us. We were starting to develop physically and having men in our one-bedroom apartment made her uneasy.

One night, while Dad, Aunt Camila, and their friends were over, Mom sat silent and watched them. Aunt Camila, who was a single mom, seemed to always be in the group. Dad was her only brother, that's why I think they were so close. Dad and Aunt Camila turned the music on and began to dance. So, we decided to dance, too. Something odd happened as one of the men who danced with me asked me out. I thought, *what is this old man thinking about to even ask me this? Was it the drinking that made it okay to ask me this stupid question?* I guess my facial gesture was enough to change his mind. Eventually they all left and Dad did not return until the next day.

We woke up the following morning and started to clean the floors. We used bleach in the bathroom because *these* men had no idea that urine belongs in the toilet and not everywhere else. Mom was disgusted by the disrespect shown to our home. She assured us this would be the last time. I confessed to her that one of the men asked me out. I don't know if she was appalled or not, but she assured me that would not happen again. "I am going to speak with your father," she said.

Mom told my dad about what had happened the last time the party ended up at our house and that she did not want this to continue. The next Friday before leaving to meet up with his buddies and Aunt Camila, an argument ensued as they both exchanged some words. This seemed to happen more so when he wanted money to decompress and indulge in beer and cards.

They would argue about how much money to take. Mom wanted to make sure she had enough money for all that she needed to provide for us. By now, Mom was pregnant with her eighth child and I felt I needed to get in the middle because the voices where getting louder. I got in the middle of this argument, acting as a shield. The next thing I knew, he reached to attempt to take money out of her hand. I was so filled with hurt and anger that this happened, I threatened to call the police.

At this point, Pablo walked in and they exchanged verbal and physical shoving while I was still in between Mom and Dad. Dad was shaking from anger and shock.

I yelled, "You won't do this again. I am calling the police." I ran to the phone, took the receiver off its hook, and pretended to talk.

He said as he panted heavily, "Forget you're my daughter," and he stood up and left the house. I was just trying to stop the argument from escalating and trying to avoid a fist fight with my teenage brother.

Dad really believed I called the police to arrest him. What I was really doing was pretending I dialed a number and pretending I was talking to someone when in reality I wasn't. Dad didn't show up that night and later we heard that he was telling his friends that his daughter, Veronica (i.e. me), threw him out of the house.

My aunt was upset at me. Finally, after three days, he came back home, but wasn't talking to me.

I later saw Aunt Camila at a party. "You did the wrong thing, little one," she said. I became angry. I eyed her up and down before I spoke. "I saw you do the same thing to your dad when he was doing the same thing to your mom and I remember verbatim the words you said."

She looked at me with such astonishment. I reminded her and said, "You said, 'do you think we're living in the old days? We're not anymore,' and you threw him against the wall before you threw him out of the house." Aunt Camila swallowed hard.

Her face was flush with shock over my recall. I continued. "Just so you know, I will do it over and over again. I will defend my mom and I will not allow anyone to mistreat her like that." I knew then, I had the voice and strength to fight for what I believed was right and that I wasn't going to change my mind or be told otherwise.

Dad got the point and stopped bringing men to the house. Now that I'm older I acknowledge that Dad was a hard-working man and what he did was his way to decompress. He never left us without food. Maybe the fight was because Mom put her foot down but whatever the case was, it didn't take away from my Dad being a loving Dad and a provider for his big family. He showed his love. He did his best and that was good enough for me. *I love you and forgive you Dad. I know you forgave me too.*

In my culture, girls were supposed to be supervised whenever we went out. My brothers scared the life out of any guy who had thoughts of dating us. I remember a boy, from our hometown in Mexico, who was interested in dating me. His dad was the one who would bring me gifts, every time he visited my parents. I guess after a certain age everyone interested in you showers you with gifts in our culture or at least that was my own experience. I already knew I shouldn't even think or even pay attention to any guy from our hometown.

MEMORIES

7th Grade–Franklin Jr., Long Beach

1985 Banning High in Wilmington

1985 Graduation 14 years old
(one month before my 15th birthday)

MEMORIES

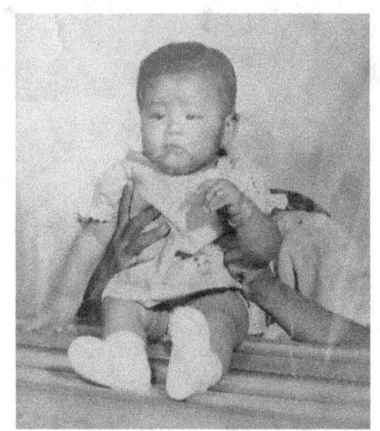
Veronica's sister Carina

Family "Donkey" pet

Veronica and Dad (Quinceanera)

MEMORIES

Queen of the Festivities in Mexico

Veronica (2nd from left) in Mexico

MEMORIES

Veronica passed citizenship test

CHAPTER 7

GOING BACK TO MEXICO

At sixteen, Mom convinced me to go back to my hometown in Mexico. She said the house that she started to build needed someone there. I didn't want to leave America because at that time, I had met someone that I was interested in dating but Mom was not comfortable leaving me here while she went back to Mexico. She still was getting used to the fact that I was getting older and was concerned that this person I had just met seemed to not leave any breathing space for me. Maybe Mom thought that by taking me with her, she would make that breathing space for me.

Before leaving for Mexico, I met Javier on a day when Mom allowed us to go out with my friend Maria's older sister, Josefina, and Alejandro. Josefina asked Mom for permission to go to a *tardeada*—an evening dance—Sunday from 6:00pm to 10:00pm. Mom said we could go if Alejandro went.

Javier was the first guy I met at this Sunday dance. He didn't seem his age. He was ten years older than me. It was interesting how seriously he seemed to want to date me. Mom said I was too young to settle down, that I should take some time to think. Perhaps she wanted to distract me and get me to understand this was moving way too fast.

When we arrived in my old hometown, it had changed and it wasn't how I remembered it. It looked old and faded. It didn't feel like home anymore and I wanted to go back to the States. Mom saw that I was having a hard time adjusting to being there and she tried to ask her friends to send their daughters to come meet me in order to make friends and feel comfortable.

Mom's friend, Margarita, came and greeted us. She introduced her daughter, Dalina, and her daughter's friend, Julia. Margarita was wearing a pretty flowered dress and a *rebozo*—a shawl—and leather sandals called *huaraches*. Dalina, who had long black hair that was braided into a ponytail, was wearing a loose-fitting pastel dress and sandals. Julia, who was shorter than Dalina and I, had short cropped wavy black hair and fair skin, was wearing a skirt and a light pink blouse. It was nice to meet them. They came to ask if I could go to a town's dance with them. I was surprised that Mom allowed me to go out with these girls.

My parents were very protective of us girls and we weren't allowed to go out on the streets. Their rules were simple—go to school, come home, do homework, chores, then watch our younger brothers while Mom makes dinner. They felt that as ladies, we should be well-behaved. They didn't want us to be out. With Mom having three more babies in succession, we were expected to help her so that she could care for us.

We arrived at the box office and there was a fellow selling tickets at the window. He wore a short sleeve white shirt and a sombrero. His pants were tight and cream colored. I couldn't see his shoes through the cutout window, but I suspect he wore huaraches (heavy duty leather sandals). My smile soon faded as he met my gaze with a barrage of questions.

"Are you from here?"

"Who are your parents?"

Before I could get the words out of my mouth, he went on."How old are you?"

Now I was irritated with him and shot back.

"Do I have to pass a test to get into this dance?"

"No," he said, "I asked because I am recruiting girls for the upcoming *Queen Of the Hometown* festival."

I said, "Not interested and my mother isn't either."

The next morning, I woke up to my grandmother cooking breakfast, but didn't see Mom. I walked towards the front courtyard when I heard voices. I looked through the front doorway and recognized the man from the box office sitting with Mom on the patio. He wore loose fitting jeans, a white tee-shirt, sandals, and his sombrero like a regular person. I heard them talking about the hometown festival.

"I don't think my daughter is interested. I'm not either especially if she has to raise funds."

"No, she won't need money," he said. He leaned back and chuckled. "This pageant is determined by votes."

Whatever else was said convinced Mom that this was ok, and I would have fun. She saw me standing behind the doorway and motioned me over. After the talk, we agreed to do it and asked what the next steps were. He said I needed to attend all the dances until the night of the voting.

We shared the news with our family. My cousin, Silvano, went into public relations manager mode. He threw a party to invite many people to meet me and to get their votes. I met many boys and girls who I became good friends with. We partied and danced and hung out a lot together. And as long as we stayed in town, Mom was ok with that. But if we wanted to go outside of town, Mom was coming with us and reminding us *who* was in charge.

I did as I was told. I went to every dance. Mom reminded me to dance with the first young man who asked. I didn't care for dancing all of the time nor with just anybody, so I asked my distant cousin (3rd or 4th cousin on my Dad's side), Paz, to always be the first to ask me.

Paz was "easy on the eyes," as the saying goes, and girls liked him a lot. I enjoyed dancing with him, and he didn't seem to mind. Mom was glad he would dance with me. It is funny to me to think how many relatives I had in that small town in Mexico. If though we weren't all related, the joke was I couldn't marry anyone there, because we were.

We were inseparable as we began to develop feelings towards one another. We did everything together—dancing, eating, partying, and just hanging out. No one seemed to mind. When we would be out together, sometimes we found ourselves holding each other's hands.

The more we would be together, the more our feelings began to show for one another. This is not something that should happen between cousins.

I remember going to the fair and he kissed me. I slapped him.

"What are you thinking?"

He looked at me with such horror.

"Paz, you're my cousin, and we should not be doing this."

He apologized and nodded.

We didn't say much as we left the fair and headed home.

After that night, we did seem to stay close. We talked more, did silly things like when he and some of his friends dressed up in girls' clothes and went chicken stealing. And, yes, we even found ourselves in those "kissing" moments, too. I liked him. He liked me. But we knew this was not possible. We were not going to be a couple.

One day, Mom took us to a *balniario* party, or a pool clubhouse party in another town. We ate and swam during the day while at night we danced. We stayed overnight because it's dangerous to travel at night in that part of town. I always felt safe with Mom.

The night came and we all went out for live music and

dinner. As I danced with Paz, right behind me I was startled by the sound of a gunshot. I whirled around and saw a man with a gun in his hand who stood over a woman on the floor. There were screams from people that ran for safety everywhere. It seemed as if time stood still before we heard sirens blaring in the distance.

The ambulances and police converged on the scene. We were all questioned by the police about what happened. Word was spreading through the crowd that the reason he shot her was because she didn't want to dance with him. I remembered what my parents taught us—it's okay to dance when asked. That bit of instruction could have saved her life. Needless to say, I was glad to be alive and with Mom. Thank God my family made it out alive.

We were getting close to the event that would crown the town queen. There was a rumor that one of the girls in the contest brought a bus full of students from her school in Teloloapan, Guerrero. We all were hoping for votes to win but that was extreme, I thought.

The day finally arrived, and the celebration of the year was tangible. One of the attractions at these festivals are the bull riding events. The newly named *Queen* rides a decorated truck, laced with fresh flowers, as she is paraded around the venue. There is a special seat for her at the bull riding event.

I remember Pablo riding a bull when I was little. It scared Mom to death when he was gored in his neck and his blood spewed everywhere. Then to learn her boys were doing this shook her.

I saw this bull rider who had been trying to get my attention during the dances but I was not interested in paying any attention to him, besides, my cousin didn't allow any space for any guy to be around me. When the bull riding event began, this guy came to offer his cowboy hat and said that his riding was dedicated to me. I didn't know him, but didn't want him to ride this bull because not even the best bull riders were riding it and the way this bull was announced, was that it was one of the meanest bulls and that it had killed a couple of bull riders in the past.

I didn't want to feel the pressure of owing him anything, so I remember saying to him to please not ride it, that I didn't want to feel responsible if anything happened to him and that he had nothing to prove to me. He still went ahead and rode the bull and exactly what we all thought was going to happen, happened.

The minute he was on the bull, the bull tried to get him off and destroy him. The bull rider got stuck and all we could see was something that looked like a cloth doll, hanging from the bull. He was kicked around and was unconscious. The men in the corral ring were trying to keep him safe and were able to run to his rescue and distract the bull. Once the bull was loose, he jumped out of the bull ring and took off running to the streets.

The bull rider was taken to get medical help and ended up on crutches for the remainder of the festivities. One thing I remember thinking, was that sometimes some men just don't think or care about their life. Life is taken lightly, and sometimes it's a scary thing. This was something I didn't want to be part of for sure. It's a dangerous sport, for the life of me I will never understand why people enjoy it.

At the start of the dance, the announcer told the crowd to vote for us, enjoy food, and dance and that the votes would be tallied up at the end of the night and we would know who would be crowned *Queen of The Town*. The festivities did not disappoint as everyone, both young and old, danced to their heart's content. During the dance, the three of us were introduced to the crowd as the contestants. We stood on the stage and waved. The announcer said the judges were about to count the votes. They sequestered the three of us to a room to count the votes in front of us, while the rest of our families, friends, and patrons waited. Silvano, my cousin, was nervously hopeful that I would win.

If I won, I was going to prank him and act disappointed in a loss.

After all the votes were counted, we knew the winner, but the judges had to be the ones to announce the winner.

Silvano saw me and asked, "Did you win?"

I passed my cousin and looked at him with great sorrow. I knew he wanted me to win.

The first judge took the microphone from the announcer. The crowd silenced themselves to listen.

"The winner with four hundred and eleven votes and the *Queen of The Town* is . . ."

It was silent as he purposefully took breaths before saying my name. My family and friends jumped for joy as they surrounded me. Mom was the first to greet me and held me tight.

CHAPTER 8

MY FIRST HUSBAND

Soon after Mom and I returned from Mexico, Javier and I resumed our intense dating relationship, seemingly picking up where we left off. He not only showered me with diamonds, balloons, and flowers, but made an effort to ensure we were always together.

Mom used to say that the man I would marry would treat me like a queen, provide a house for us, and love me and my family. Even if I was treated like a queen, Mom always made sure to instill in us that we needed to be independent and able to work and care for ourselves. At the time, I thought that Javier was fulfilling all the things Mom used to say to me about my future husband. I wasn't sure that I wanted to marry Javier but I knew that if I wanted to honor my parents (in Latino culture, it is frowned upon if you leave home unmarried and it's seen as dishonoring your parents) and be free from the smothering I was feeling from my parents, I had to marry him. Whenever Javier and I went out, Mom chaperoned. We wanted to be close but it's hard to do when your Mom is always there. We would dance just to be close. I felt restricted and that I wasn't able to think for myself. My only hope, or so I thought, was to get married in order to leave home in an honorable way and gain the freedom I sought to be able to think for myself and make my own decisions. Nevertheless, Mom thought Javier was moving too fast, showing up early and staying way late, giving me gifts and showing me too much attention. Despite the 10-year age gap between us, we were engaged and married within a year and a half of my return from Mexico.

Soon after we were married, I started my new job at South Gate Middle School as an office assistant and then things sure did change. Javier became isolative, manipulative, and controlling. I would want to be involved in family gatherings and he would just be distant and anti-social. It felt like he was disrespectful to my family. I didn't know how to process this. Who could I turn to for help? I kept wondering where was the man that showered me with attention and gifts and was supposed to treat me like a queen?

I decided to get counsel from Pablo and Dario. Both were just an external representation of my internal conflict.

"You wanted to marry him, you have to deal with the good and the bad," Pablo said. "You should have thought about all of this before you married him."

He was right. I should have thought about it more. How was I supposed to know that this was how Javier was going to become? He showed no signs of this when he was sending those extravagant gifts.

Dario was more supportive on my behalf.

I needed to do something. I needed to get us help. I reached out to the priest who married us, but that didn't make the situation any better. I tried to get help from a Jehovah's Witness Bible study. That did nothing. I tried a counselor, who made a statement that more or less said that I was the mature one and he was the child.

Javier was feeling as though I was pressuring him to spend time with my family, but I wanted him to know how important family was to me. I wanted things to go back to the way they were when he was "chasing me down."

My family life got even worse. My father was murdered. That traumatic experience seemed to be the start of a horrible chain of events.

At this time, Dad was working as a day laborer. Each day after work, he and several other co-workers as well as neighbors and friends would meet up at a Long Beach park to play basketball. On this one particular day, he happened onto a fight between a man and a woman.

Dad tried to calm the man down, but it only upset him even more. However, and whatever way my dad attempted to de-escalate the situation did not help. The angry man went to his truck, grabbed an ice pick, came back and stabbed Dad below his heart. The pick hit an artery. My injured Dad made it to the door of someone he knew who lived near the park who was from our hometown, knocked, and asked for help.

By the time the paramedics arrived, Dad had lost a lot of blood. They got him to a hospital and put him on life-support. The doctors told us that the amount of blood loss and lack of oxygen made this situation grave.

A month later, in a vegetative state, we agreed to pull the plug. He was gone. A random act of violence, by an angry man, took away the man we all loved. I will forever be grateful for the afternoon before my dad's attack. He stopped by my house. I opened the door and was surprised he stopped by because he didn't normally do that.

When I opened the door, I saw his face full of radiant light. I said, "Dad, have you been out in the sun? You're shining and your face looks pink." He said he worked on a few of the plants in his front porch.

I asked why he stopped by?

He said, "I just wanted to see you and say I love you and goodbye."

I said, "I love you too Dad." I gave him a big hug and kiss on his pink, glossy cheek and he left.

That same night I had a nightmare that my dad was in the front porch of my house when a car pulled up and shot him right in his heart. I woke up screaming saying, "We have to get my dad in the house he just got shot"

Even though I was awake and knew it was a bad dream I couldn't stop crying. Today, I realized that God's grace was given to me even when I didn't follow him or really know about him. I finally fell back to sleep and woke up to go to work. At around mid-morning I was called into one of the conference rooms and my co-worker, Olive gave me the news. My brother Adan was enrolled at this school where I worked. I summoned him out of class and drove straight to the hospital.

Javier was still non-supportive during this awful time. My family needed me. Mom needed me. Soon after Dad's death, Mom moved to a new place so that my brothers weren't reminded of the tragedy. They were getting older and Mom felt a different house and a change of scenery, would do them all good. This was good because a fresh start meant new friends and new environment.

Carina was still at home and had gotten a new job but couldn't take the boys to school. My brothers were supposed to be taking the bus, but for whatever reason, they didn't always catch it on time and were forced to walk a long way. Mom bought Adan a truck to help take him and our younger brothers to school. This worked well. Even when Victorio, and his friends needed a ride, Adan was there.

But once again, another tragic event happened to my family. Victorio and his friends, along with the friend's older brothers, asked Adan to give them a ride to a house. What Adan did not know was that Victorio and his friends had some issues with the young man who lived at this house. Adan didn't want to go because he was with his girlfriend. However, he changed his mind because he didn't want any teasing from Victorio's friends and went ahead and took them. That decision changed my brothers lives and ours too.

When they got to the house, Victorio, his friends, and older brothers, got out of the truck and went up the driveway to the house. As they approached the house, the person that they had an issue with, came out with a knife. The escalation reached a boiling point. It was at this point that one of Victorio's friend's older brothers, pulled out a gun and started shooting. The young man whose house they went to, was killed by the gunfire. Everyone ran, but the police were able to get all, except the actual shooter. Charges were filed against my brothers and their friends. Adan, who was sixteen, got fifteen years to life in prison and was charged with first-degree murder because of the decision he made to go in front of a jury. Victorio, who was fourteen at the time, received ten years in prison. Victorio got less jail time but they were both charged as adults.

The stress was mounting, and I wanted to be with Mom. The death of her husband was hard enough and to make matters worse, her two sons were in jail. Javier's behavior was not helping and the guilt I felt for not being with my family was heavy on me. I had reached my breaking point. I told him I wanted a divorce.

I was put off by his response. He began making threats of hurting himself and me too. I was naïve to think that he would actually do these things until the threats turned to reality as he began punching, kicking, and headbutting walls each time I brought up the subject of divorce. It wasn't long before I started thinking that if he was willing to do this to himself, what would stop him from doing this to me. I didn't want things to get this bad where he was hurting himself and he could potentially hurt me. I recanted my divorce threats, but it didn't matter and it didn't change him. He continued to be dismissive, non-social, and irrational. As a result, we lived our lives as co-habitants and not as husband and wife as we had vowed to be.

I was anxious to jumpstart my quasi-single-still married-but-wanted-to-be-divorced-life and one night, my friends Blanca, Margie, and I went to a club where Pepe Reyes, a disc jockey from a popular Spanish-speaking radio station, Radio Caliente 1430AM, came up to me and clued me in on a contest. He asked if I was interested in a runway contest where the winner would get an all-expense paid photo-shoot trip to Cancun. He also stated that the winner would be in a music video for a popular Spanish-singing music group, *Los Tigres del Norte*.

I thought, *why not? This could be fun.* As it turned out, I won! I was excited. I had never known that this could have happened to me. This led to more worldly opportunities like modeling jobs for magazines, CD covers, and more music videos. The success I had now moved into made it easier for me to not think of Javier.

He sensed that I was moving on since I was not coming home and staying at Mom's more often than not, but he still tried to keep me under his rules.

Each day that passed, Javier could see that I was moving on as if I wasn't married to him. He continued to try and convince me to move back home, where he said I belonged.

When I came back from filming a video in Cancun, I got introduced to a modeling agency where I met Mia. She was already working for the agency and I was super excited to get to know the ins-and-outs of the business. We had conversations over the course of the next few weeks as she kept getting jobs while I was still learning the ropes.

I ran into her after she had just gotten work at a small music company and she suggested I apply for a job as a background singer. The company she was working for was having auditions for a band later in the month and since I loved to sing, I thought, this was something I could try. I decided to take some piano and singing classes at a local junior college to be ready for that audition. After a few short vocal lessons, I went to the audition, and did my best. Things went well enough that they offered me a position with Mia as a back-up singer for Roma, who was the lead singer.

Mia and I became good friends with each other as we spent a lot more time together. As a trusted friend, I told her about my rocky marital status, and she was very empathetic. When I told her that I had no desire of going back to live with Javier by myself, we came up with a plan that benefitted both of us. She would move in with me, renting a room so that I would not have to be alone in the house with Javier. The idea was that when I wasn't staying at my mother's place, Mia would stay with me in the house.

Javier's manipulative skills led him to say he was moving out, but I soon learned he was building an add-on to the house to be close by. He would come and go as he pleased, while we were there, and it was just another way to show he had the control over me. If I didn't bring up the divorce, Javier seemed to be okay with the living arrangements. I know he wanted us to stay married, but that was not something I wanted anymore.

Mom was concerned about my safety because, that's what moms do, and she implored me not to upset him. I felt safe when Mia was there. It was clear to me that he was not going to leave. Even though I would lock the doors, he would simply use his key and let himself in. I am sure he felt in control.

One day, I went by the house and didn't see his car in the driveway. *Maybe I will take a quick shower, grab some of my things, and leave,* I thought. I locked the door and went into the shower. Afterwards, I went into the bedroom to get dressed, and out of nowhere, Javier was there. He had a look I had not seen before. He shoved me into my closet and forced himself on me.

We hadn't been intimate, in nearly nine months. I didn't try to fight him off of me. I could hear my mother's words—*don't make him upset*—so I let him do what he did. I forced myself to separate my mind from my body. He finished, got dressed, and left. I blamed myself for allowing this to happen by being careless (at least that's what I told myself at the time but I now know that was a lie).

I also made the decision to not tell anyone about this, pretend that it never happened, and move on as if everything was normal. I kept telling myself that I was going to have to fight through this until I could get out of this marriage.

Three months later, Javier and I talked. I was determined to let him know that I was done with him, and the divorce had to happen. We would do this "song-and-dance" where he promised to be better if I didn't leave or he would threaten to hurt himself and me if I did leave. I couldn't keep living like this.

It just so happened that on the next day, I received a call from the hospital. After he had gone to work, he somehow got his hand caught in a grinding machine. I arrived at the hospital and found him in one of the waiting bays in the emergency room. He cried and said, "don't leave me" and that he needed me. I cried, too. I just kept thinking this was my fault.

He went to therapy soon to regain strength and function in his hand. I agreed to help him in his recovery with basic things as long as he didn't stay in the house and stayed in his outside addition. Not once during that time, did we talk about divorcing one another. I stayed at our house only when Mia was there. Other times, I stayed with Mom.

While he recuperated, I continued working my day job as an office assistant to continue paying the bills. At night, I reconnected with my friends and began returning to the music scene with Mia and Roma. This was needed as I had to take a break from caring for Javier. But we needed more money since he wasn't working. I ended up getting a hostess job for a local Japanese restaurant. The pace was steady, and it made the nights go by fast. I saw many of the same customers, but one kept showing up when I was working.

He was Japanese and his name was Kaori. He was a kind and gentle man. He wasn't tall but he wasn't short either. He had black hair, was clean cut, and wore a black polo and black pants the night we met. We introduced ourselves to each other and started to chat. He was soft-spoken and sweet. After a few visits to the restaurant, he asked me out, and I said yes. It wasn't long after that we began dating.

Even though I was still married, I felt something different with Kaori than I did with Javier.

I filled him on my life story, the ups and downs, the good and bad. Kaori never judged me. He was considerate, patient, and supportive. Time moved along and we became more serious and it seemed like things picked up in the music aspect of my life, too. My group recorded a demo and went on tour in Northern California, Colorado, Baja, Texas, Mexico City, and some cities in the U.S. I liked this because I didn't have to be around Javier. I stayed with Mom when I was home and he was none the wiser about my interactions with another man.

Kaori and I were a "couple" and I wanted Kaori to meet Mom. He agreed and off to Mom's we went. We walked inside her house and they hit it off instantly. This made me very happy. But I knew something had to happen for me and Javier to get divorced. I was ready to move on with my life. A life with Kaori was all I could see. I needed to muster up the strength and courage to file the paperwork.

My heart loved to hear Kaori say things like, "*When I marry you, I want your mom to have a house next to us*" or, "*I respect that lady for all she means to you and what she's gone through.*" I felt some kind of way every time he spoke.

It wasn't long after Kaori and Mom met that she started feeling sick and had some discomfort in her back. On non-rehearsal days, I would take Mom to Baja, Mexico to see a doctor. She preferred the doctors there as opposed to California, and not to mention, money went a long way there, too.

Kaori was so understanding and supportive, whereas my husband was the exact opposite. He guilted me so much. He would say things like, "Why are you always taking care of her? Why does it have to be you?"

I was upset at his selfishness.

We learned from the Mexican doctor that Mom had bronchitis, but the weight loss was unexplainable.

We decided to go back to California for additional testing. She saw more doctors and they ran more tests, as the weight-loss continued with no answers seemingly in sight. It took a few weeks before we knew exactly what was wrong with her.

Talking to Javier about Mom's health was a waste. Kaori, though, was encouraging and giving advice, and words of love that was a balm to my hurting soul. He made time to listen to me and I was grateful to have him in my life.

But the happiness would not last.

We both had some free time in our schedules and we got together. He said he had something to share with me. The tone in his voice was not like anything I had ever heard from him. He was distracted, constantly rubbing his hands together, as he sat with me. I rubbed his back to comfort him. I did it for me, too, as I was getting restless.

"The timing hadn't been right recently for me to share this with you," he said.

"I understand."

"I care deeply for you and want you to know that this has been stressing me out."

I could see the grief on his face. Whatever it was he held inside; it was taking a toll on him.

"Talk babe . . . I am listening."

"I am married, but going through a divorce."

His words cut me. My mouth dropped as he continued with another bombshell.

"I also have a two-year old daughter."

I began to shake. I was crushed. My heart ached as I began to process what I had heard. He might have said her name, but I shut down. Was I the reason for him divorcing his wife? If not, he would have to go through this divorce alone. I didn't want to be caught up in the drama.

We stayed together from that night until the next afternoon. We agreed to go our separate ways. We were devasted. The heartbreak was palpable.

The days turned into weeks, I was still following my same routine—work, music, work, taking care of Mom. I missed Kaori. I could still hear his voice, the smell of his cologne, and reminisce over our long talks.

One day, at Mom's, Kaori called. My heart leapt to my throat when I heard his voice. He wanted to know how Mom and family were. He asked to visit my mother.

"*I want to see you,*" I thought, as I asked Mom if it was okay for him to see her. She said yes and he came by for breakfast. The three of us talked like old times. He then asked if I wanted to meet his daughter, Kaya. I wasn't sure how I felt. But I loved and missed him.

Kaori could see I was apprehensive so he suggested a lunch date. I was conflicted with so many emotions, on one hand, I didn't want to keep reliving the pain of our break-up again, but maybe there was something hopeful between us again.

The day came for the meet-and-greet with Kaya. When I got in the car and Kaori turned the car on, the music playing caught my heart. It was a lullaby and the words said, "Jesus Loves me, Yes, I know for the Bible tells me so." We decided to go to a local Japanese restaurant.

We walked in and sat at a table near the window. Kaya was cute with pudgy cheeks. Her hair was black with a bob cut and well-kept.

Kaori took my chair out, and set it under me. He sat and smiled. He properly introduced me to Kaya, and I smiled as she took my hand. *She must be comfortable with me to take my hand*, I thought.

We saw each other a few more times after that and it was always a relaxed and nice feeling. But conflict knocked on my door with regularity. In the ten years of being married to Javier we never had kids and here this child was relaxed with me. One thing my heart desired was to be married with the husband who would have my first and only children. I kept trying to envision myself being a step-mom and compromising my heart's desires. This was the conflict of my heart. As hard as it was I needed to make the right decision and needed to stay true to myself. If I decided to stay with Kaori I would have to compromise my heart desires and the question I kept asking myself was if I was going to be okay with letting those desires go or would I later regret and live wondering what if? This decision seemed easy when I would counsel my heart's desires but it was easier said than done. I loved this man and I wrestled back and forth until one day I could see and hear that voice clearly.

While working at the Japanese restaurant, I met a lady who worked at a night club. She said she made a good amount of money and that I should check it out.

My first thought was *is this a strip club*? I had no desire for that line of work. She kept insisting on the money angle and the amount I could make. I deliberated with my heart and mind and after assuring it wasn't what I thought, I became intrigued and decided to check into it.

At this point, I had taken a leave of absence from the office administrative job with the Los Angeles School District and I needed cash. When I had the chance, I went to the address the lady I met had given me on Foothill Blvd in Pasadena. It was a brightly lit place on the outside, but it had disco flashing lights on stage and colored lights on the rest of the club and music playing when I walked inside. I saw women dancing with bikini bathing suits on, which put some ease in my steps as I walked to the bar. I asked for the manager, Mitch, and the bartender nodded his head in his direction.

Mitch was about six feet tall, had a white beard, and looked like Santa Claus except he had no fat belly. He was very friendly and kind. He wore jewelry around his neck that made me think he had money. Judging from the amount of people there, I could see why. He invited me to his office and interviewed me.

Whatever I said, he liked, as he offered me a job starting that night. I needed the money and the time flexibility to care for Mom was an added bonus. So, it was a no-brainer to accept it.

One night at the night club, right before closing time, I met Ron. He was cheerful, charming, handsomely square jawed, and nice. I didn't have any romantic thoughts about him, but there was something about him. We talked and got to know a little bit about each other. He was witty and respectful. He said that he would like to see me again. "I will be here next week, same time," I said.

Sure enough, the next week, he was there and also brought his friends, Jason and Kurt. Jason seemed to look angry and Kurt was nice and relaxed. They sat themselves at an unoccupied table. I saw Ron go to the bar.

I approached Jason and asked, "Is everything okay with you?

He looked at me and said, "I don't want to be here." Kurt looked at him and gave Jason a dismissive shake of the head.

"Why?" I asked.

He tipped his head in Ron's direction and said, "Because my friends were supposed to be giving me a ride to get my car. We went to a football game and carpooled there. Now that the game is over, we are here. I just wanted to get to my car and go home."

By then, Ron had walked to the table and filled me in on the rest of the story. "I remembered you were working tonight, and I wanted to keep my promise to see you like we said next week, same time, same place," he said. They sipped their drinks and as we continued to talk.

Ron pulled me aside and asked that I give Jason a private dance. I agreed to do so as it meant more money for me.

When I took Jason's hand and asked him to follow me, he was surprised and didn't seem to understand what was happening. When I told him that we were going to the VIP lounge so we could be alone for a private dance, he hesitated and expressed he was not happy with Ron doing this. I could tell he liked me, but that he was uncomfortable with the whole idea of getting a private dance.

I would learn later that my intuition was right in that he liked me, but that he felt that by getting a private dance, I would assume that he was just like all the other guys that came into the club and was only interested in me physically and would lose any hope of getting to know me or getting together with me on a date outside of the club.

I assured him that everything was ok, and that we would do more talking than me dancing. He seemed a little at ease with this and agreed to it. We spent the time together and talked some more.

My First Husband

When the night was over and it was time for everyone to leave, Jason took out a pen and wrote his number on a napkin. He said:

"I know you're not going to call me."

"Do you like surprises?" I responded.

"Yes, I am good with surprises," he said as he shifted in his seat.

"Well... I might just surprise you."

And with that, they all stood up, said goodbye, as Jason trailed. It looked like Jason didn't seem bothered anymore.

It took me two weeks after that exchange to squash my nervousness and call Jason. Aside from my internal questions of whether or not he liked me or if I liked him, I still was dealing with Mom's health, Javier issues and Kaori/Kaya feelings.

I decided to call the number on the ratty napkin. It was a two-way pager number. I got his greeting and left a short message without leaving my phone number. Purposefully. Hey, if he wanted to know me, he'd have to do the work and come see me in person.

When I went to work a few days later, to my surprise, there was Jason. I was told he waited for me for two hours. When I finally passed by him, he called my attention, but there was another girl next to him, and I didn't want to be rude, so I just waved and kept on walking.

But he stopped me right away and gave the girl a look as if to say, "Thanks for the company but I'm here to talk to her."

He told me that she approached him and started talking to him. He made it clear to her that he was there looking for me. He told her that if I didn't show up, he would leave and that he had no interest talking to anyone else. She told him, "I'll stay here until she shows up."

When we had a chance to talk, he immediately told me that he only came to get my phone number and that he was leaving after that. I already knew that I liked him, but didn't know where this was going to go or if he was even mature enough for me to be interested in him. I wanted to give him a chance, so I went ahead and wrote down my phone number and gave it to him. He left immediately after that.

He called the next day, Saturday, and we decided to do lunch. I told him I would be at my mother's house, gave him the address, and got ready. I liked that we were doing an informal lunch. No need for being serious and what-not.

Jason pulled up in a bright green Ford Explorer truck. It seemed like it was right off of the dealership lot. He got out, opened my door, and ushered me inside the truck. It wasn't long before he returned to the driver side and we were off to eat.

We chatted briefly and got to the restaurant quickly. It was a Mexican food restaurant in Santa Monica. The conversation seemed to steer towards relationships. I did share with him that I was married, and some more details and he was non-judgmental. We finished our lunch and went for a walk. It was nice to just be me again. We returned back to the truck and he mentioned that he was going to church the next day.

Something tugged my heart as I listened to him speak about his church. "Love for you to visit," he said. *This is what I have been waiting for*, I thought. I had been looking for a place to worship. I took a few flyers from a church near Mom's house but never went. I agreed that in a few weeks, I would visit his church with him.

On a Saturday night, I decided to let Jason know I would go to church with him the next day. It seemed after I made that decision, there were dark forces attempting to stop me from going. Earlier in the week, I had sprained a ligament in my knee. Mom's health was still not good, then Mia woke up with terrible stomach pains that same Saturday night. We went to urgent care and after the examinations, she was sent home with prescriptions we needed to get from the pharmacy. It was getting to be the morning time, and I was fighting the urge to succumb to the calls of sleep. I wanted to be awake for Jason when he picked me up for Sunday service.

When Jason arrived at my house, I went to the door to greet him only to see Javier pulling up in his car at the same time. *Why is he here . . . ?*

I got to the screen door and said to Jason, "Trust me and go wait for me at Mom's house," which happened to be around the corner from my house. He left and I waited a little. He probably thought, "Who is that man?"

I don't think Javier saw me open the door and he went on to the side gate and into the back of the house. He used to plant all kinds of vegetables in the back and if he was in the back, he was always doing something with his vegetables like watering, picking them, or planting.

I took that opportunity to leave and go meet Jason right outside Mom's house. I was ready and went to church. When I hopped into the truck with Jason he asked, "What just happened?"

I told him that I didn't want to take any chances with Javier and that I didn't know what would happen if he saw me leaving with him. He seemed to understand and we left it at that.

We drove for about an hour to his church. When I walked into church, the worship song I heard was, "Jesus loves me, this I know for the Bible tells me so" or something like that. I knew I was there at the right time to hear the message.

The sermon was about baggage that we all bring to relationships. The pastor talked about how we carry baggage around from relationship to relationship. He emphasized on how we didn't have to carry that entire heavy burden around and that God could take that burden off our shoulders and that we just had to trust and believe. It was as if this message was tailor made for me. I left the service that day feeling hopeful and at peace.

CHAPTER 9

A GLIMPSE OF REAL LOVE

Kaori was always so kind, caring, and thoughtful. He was a man of God who showed me love when I needed it the most. He penned me many letters, I'm sharing to show his heart for me:

Veronica,

I had been holding on to this card for a long time. When I read it, I wanted to give it to you. However, after I heard that you were with someone else, it didn't seem right to give it to you. Not because my feelings changed, but out of respect to you and to him.

After talking to you yesterday, you asked that I not make any stories. It made me think that it's alright for me to share this card with you. All I'm doing is being honest and sincere. There is no fault in that. This card is very close to my heart. What I realized reading it was that I learned how to love because of you. What I believe was love was only the beginning. You, Vero were my first true love. It really did shock me but thinking about it deeply it's true. Thank you and God for that. I look forward to hearing about all the wonderful, exciting things in your life now.

Ai shite imasu ("I love you" in Japanese), Kaori.

Veronica,

Love . . . a small word for such a complex emotion. There is no simple explanation for it, because love is made up of many things. It cannot be measure, because it is a feeling. All of the money in the world cannot buy love to be earned. It does not happen by wishing, it must come about naturally.

Love is not an instantaneous emotion, but something that grows slowly between two people, maturing with time. Once love has reached maturity, there is no stronger bond between two people.

To love someone means being comfortable and at ease with them, sharing confidences knowing that they will be understood and held in trust. It means respecting each other's dignity and never being demanding, but rather being willing to give, and accepting that which is given, graciously and with love.

A Glimpse of Real Love

To love someone means having a genuine concern for them, being able to sense that something is wrong without being told. It is understanding the other person's problems, moods, and "hang-ups," and accepting all of them even if you don't quite understand. It is excusing their faults, because you know that their good points far outweigh the bad.

Love is always being there for each other with a shoulder to cry on, to give support when confidence levels are low, to give helpful advice when it is asked for, to know when to be silent and just listen, or to give cheerful words of encouragement.

Love is sharing the good and the bad, the hopes and the dreams, the amusing times and the serious times. It is doing things together yet leaving room for each to grow as an individual.

How do I know these things about love? Because this is the kind of love you have given to me and the kind of love I feel for you.

I am blessed with your love, and I strive to become an even better person and always be deserving of your love, because I truly love you as I have never loved before. It's true.

Ai shite imasu, Kaori

His letters were encouraging as they came at a time when Mom's health was taking a turn for the worse. We had gotten news from the doctor about her test results. It revealed stage IV stomach cancer and she only had a few months to live. That diagnosis crippled us and we didn't want to believe it.

Mom was a fighter. She did not just sit around and take her lumps. She had hope and she was determined to fight. I know she is who I get my determination from. She had stopped eating solid foods and was only drinking liquids, but it wasn't long after that, that liquids were being rejected by her body, too. Mom heard about an herbalist woman in Seattle, Washington, that could help. Our expectation was raised when it was said to us that this lady could cure Mom.

We bought plane tickets and arranged to fly out to Seattle. It had been a couple months since I had begun seeing Jason. We agreed to continue dating and being exclusive but I needed to leave with Mom to Seattle. He understood and was supportive. As for Javier, the divorce process was going to have to wait ... again.

It was difficult for Mom to walk and stand independently because of the pain. I was glad the airlines gave her a wheelchair to board and deplane. I held her hand when we flew. Mom, my best friend, was frail and sick and there was nothing I could do for her. As I sat with her, I could hear in my head *"You are strong, and you will get through this* and *you can do all things."*

I was glad I had spoken with Kaori before we left. I told him about mom's situation. Even though we were not seeing each other anymore, I was glad he would call to check on her.

Soon, he would send cards and letters that would encourage me during this difficult time.

Mi Alma, (My soul) He learned this word from me.

I write this card and the attached letter to you on this Easter day when God gave us a way to be with him. He took away our sins and forgave us. I ask for your forgiveness and to support my walk to reach God.

I love you forever . . . that's where you'll always be.
Happy Easter, Kaori

We arrived in Seattle and were picked up by May, the herbalist, and her husband, David. He was broad-shoulder and muscular. He wore a short sleeve button down shirt and grey dockers. May was tall and plump with a head of short silver hair, fair skin, and blue eyes. She was wearing a turquoise top and black pants.

 We arrived at their place. It was small and surrounded with trees that prevented people from looking in or out. The front of the house was outfitted with large bay windows. The driveway was unfinished and rocky. We got inside and the first thing May did was check Mom's blood count and took a urine sample. She also mentioned that she needed Mom off the morphine because it was damaging her liver.

Being there gave me lots of quiet time, and I would write my thoughts during the day. I would pray for guidance and strength. A few days after our arrival in Seattle, I received a package with an English/Spanish Bible from Jason. His message was, "Veronica, I thought you would enjoy this version. When I saw it, I had to get it for you. Read it faithfully and use God's strength to get you through life. I love you very much my love."

Daily, May checked Mom's blood count. It seemed to improve, and we took that as a good sign.

This was a good sign according to May. Mom would rest a lot and was in bed most of the time throughout the day. I would help her outside and we would sit in the back yard every day as I read the Bible to her. Mom liked that and was happy to hear me read it for her.

Mom's stomach was still very bloated. She would make groaning sounds and would ask me to lie underneath her to hold her and massage her stomach to make it feel better because she was in constant pain. I remember thinking that there was a day when Mom cared for me the same way I was caring for her now. This was a surreal moment. I was taking care of her like she did for me when I was a baby. May made it clear—no medication, meaning no morphine for Mom. This was repeated for days on end. It was hard not to oblige Mom, but we wanted to obey May's instructions.

One day, Mom asked for food. We thought that was great news since she hadn't eaten in weeks. As her blood count increased, hope was being increased, too. The pain kept on increasing and Mom kept asking for relief. I wanted her to live but I didn't want her to live with this pain. It was tough watching her suffer.

Many times, I broke down and cried inconsolably as I knelt beside her bed. This time, I couldn't take it anymore and I gave her the morphine. I knew it wasn't right, because that's what May said. But I needed her to feel better. I cried out to God and surrendered Mom to Him, after I realized how selfish I was being.

The price for keeping her here was seeing her suffer. Mom had enough suffering in her life. I did not need to add more. If it was in my power, I wasn't going to allow that to continue anymore. I knew Mom was fighting for her life because of us. She knew we weren't letting her go just yet. It was at this moment when I finally let her go. I accepted what the reality was, and what reality was going to be. God in His mercy gave Mom comfort and peace.

When she finally knew the fight was over, she told me to make sure to convey a message to my brothers and sisters. She said to tell them that, "It's good to work hard but to never forget to come home to enjoy the fruit of their hard work, to make sure to share and enjoy time with their families just like the verses in the book of Proverbs 23:4-5 (NLT) says,

> *Don't wear yourself out trying to get rich. Be wise enough to know when to quit. In the blink of an eye wealth disappears.*

Mom worried for me, but she knew I was fine and that I would be okay. In the following days, she had this peace and it was like she was just waiting for her Heavenly Father to come get her. Peace came over her and she left us in God's hands, she knew we would be okay.

Before she passed, I asked May to please give us a ride to the beach, because that was something Mom enjoyed. It was a place that brought her peace. When we were there she just stared at the ocean and looked very peaceful. I waited and sat next to her. My heart was at peace knowing that we were doing all that we could do up until that point.

We got home, I helped her from the car to her bed so she could rest. By the time we got to the front door, Mom lost consciousness. I thought she died but she hadn't left us yet. I guess she was holding on to see Carina one more time since the two of us were taking turns taking care of her and she would be coming soon to take my place.

Jason called nightly to check on us. He prayed with me and I was so glad for his kindness, which was keeping me strong.

Carina arrived to help Mom and I went back to California. I had to sort out some stuff. As I was taking care of things for Mom, Carina called and said she had gone home to be with the Lord.

We made arrangements to bring her back home to be buried next to Dad. At the funeral, many family and friends, including, Kaori and Jason, showed their love and support during this difficult time. Kaori sent flowers, too. I was being shown by God that my family and I were loved.

I didn't know then that this was the beginning of my spiritual walk with God. Mom, who was my best friend, was gone and God didn't want me to suffer alone. He came to fill that empty void in my heart. He came to love me, to hold me, to comfort me at the right, and perfect time. He had always been there, right by my side. He could only come to reside in me if I would open the door to my heart and accept him into my life.

After Mom's death this song below was His gift to me. A song that brought healing to my heart, closure and acceptance of Mom's death. A true gift from God. I've never been a writer or composer of music. This is the first song and only song I've ever written. I could hear the melody and the lyrics coming from my heart and out of my mouth with tears streaming down my face as I sat inside my car in a parking lot structure.

"Recuerdo Eterno"
(Eternal Memory)

Recuerdos estaran eternamente aqui.
(Memories will always be eternally here.)

Y tu te quedaras en mi hasta el fin.
(And you will stay in me until the end.)

Chorus: Le pido al corazon que deje de sufrir, porque con el dolor no podra mas seguir.
(I ask the heart to stop suffering, because with the pain it can't go on.)

Le digo que lo acepte y vuelva a renacer, pero el corazon no lo puede entender.
(I tell it to accept it and come back to life, but the heart can't seem to understand.)

Recuerdos estaran eternamente aqui. Y tu te quedaras en mi hasta el fin.
(Memories will eternally be here, and you will stay in me until the end.)

El dia que te fuiste. Muy sola me quede.
(The day you left. I was very lonely.)

Y el recuerdo solo de ese atardecer.
(And just the memory of that evening.)

El dia que te fuiste. Muy trizte me quede.
(The day you left. I was very sad.)

Y los recuerdos solo, me hacen renacer.
(Your memories now make me come alive.)

Quisiera yo tener tus brazos otra vez.
(I wish I had your arms again.)

Porque sin tu presencia me voy a enloquecer.
(Because without your presence I will go insane.)

Le pido al corazon que deje de sufrir.
(I ask the heart to stop suffering.)

Porque con el dolor no podra mas seguir.
(Because with the pain it won't be able to go on.)

Le digo que lo acepte y vuelva a renacer.
(I ask it to accept it and come alive again.)

Pero el corazon no puede entender.
(But the heart can't understand.)

Y los recuerdo solo, me hacen renacer.
(Your memories now make me come alive.)
*****

A Glimpse of Real Love

Kaori's card to us,

Veronica, Carina, Coco, and Gavian.

When more than one heart bears the weight of a sorrow, then all hearts shall find a way to peace. With Deepest Sympathy.

Your mother's love lives within my heart forever as well. Her spirit and yours are in my prayers.

Love, Kaori

Kaori's last letter.

This letter arrived on my birthday three weeks after my mother's funeral.

HAPPY BIRTHDAY!!

From all of my heart, I want to wish you the very best Birthday ever. It gives me faith that the world is a good place knowing that kind, loving people such as you are born. With your understanding of true love, in its many forms, be happy that so much of it rains upon you. I know that the heavens pour its raindrops of love down on you especially strong this year.

I am a very fortunate person to know what our dreams and goals are. My hope and prayers for you are that on this wonderful day, you are now one step closer to obtaining them. I hope your dreams shine ever so brighter now that you have God on your side. We both know that with him leading us, we can truly be happy and complete. How wonderful that we can talk this way to each other now! Your faith makes mine stronger.

I hope you like the gifts. The picture is from Kaya, of course. We still talk about you together. I think that she has a special understanding, even as small as she was, of just how precious you are to me. The hat, as I mentioned to you, is from both of us. We got it down at that store where we got last summer's shorts and hat. You should see my shorts this year, they're crazy! (Every summer Kaori would buy a new pair of swim trunks).

Last but not least, is my present to you. I know you will love it! It is actually being mailed to me as we speak. I apologize for not timing it right, but these shipment things take ridiculously long. No excuse, though. When I receive it, I will mail it out to you.

After seeing you, I had such a flood of emotions and thoughts. I care about you so much it's incredible even to me sometimes. I feel lucky though, because I think most people *don't get to experience it. I wish the best for you, my love. Don't ever settle for anything less. I told you often, "With the sorrow and pain you've experienced in your life, God is going to give you so much Love and Happiness". I truly believe that, and I believe in you too.*

Once again, happy birthday, mi alma and God bless. Kaya sends lots of kisses and so do I.

When my birthday present arrived, he called me and asked if we could see each other. He also said he understood if I didn't want to. He said if my answer was no, he would mail the present to me.

I asked Jason what he thought? At first, I was going to say no because Jason and I were starting to take this relationship seriously. But the other side of me wanted to tell Kaori how much appreciation I had for him.

I thought that this man deserved to know how much I really appreciated all that he did for me and I wanted him to know how special he was to me and my family. I wanted him to know how grateful I was to have met him. I couldn't leave with that last memory of him at Mom's funeral. I wanted to hear his thoughts and wanted to share mine. I wanted to tell him why I thought our relationship couldn't continue.

We met on an afternoon in the lobby of New Ontani in downtown LA. This place was one of our favorite places, where we would have lunch at the sushi bar. Next to the sushi bar was the Japanese garden. Kaori and I had lots to talk about. We both were happy and hopeful for what the future had to offer us.

We both trusted that God had bigger plans for us. Later we walked to the Japanese garden. It was then that he handed me a box with my gift. I couldn't believe the piece of jewelry he bought me, because a few weeks back I had seen the exact necklace in a catalog and had made a mental note that I would buy it for myself. He didn't even know it was something I had my eye on, but he did know my taste.

This is not an everyday ordinary necklace. Only two people so close to each other's heart can connect this way. This necklace is a heart pendant with the footprints message engraved on it. It was a very appropriate gift, that had meaning and a message from God. It will always be special to me because of what it means to me, and because it was the last gift from someone that showed me what love looked like and from someone who loved me well during the brief time we had together.

Kaori and I understood that we were meant to only share a season together. It was hard to leave each other; we knew this was the last time. We cried and prayed. We left and called each other's special names one last time, as we drove away. Our hearts will always have a special place for each other. Even though it was hard to meet one last time, we knew we had to do it for each other because it brought closure for both of us. We could both move on and start a new relationship with a clean slate.

And after ten long years of enduring, fighting, and preparing, the divorce was finalized and I was free to run my life with God by my side.

CHAPTER 10

I FOUND LOVE

I have experienced years of pure, beautiful, wonderful, and amazing love. In 1999, I married my amazing and loving husband, Jason. After our honeymoon, I decided to give and surrender my life to God, my Savior, Jesus Christ. In the past ten years, Christ has given me the love I always hoped and looked for, the kind of love that makes me feel unconditionally loved, safe, and complete, just like the kind of love my mother gave and wanted me to have.

God gave me a glimpse of His love through my mother, Kaori, and others who crossed my path. I now know that He has sent each one of us to deliver His message of love. He does this through different people who have found Him and have accepted His gift of love. This is the reason we're put on this earth, so that we can show His love, bring hope, and shine His light to others. In doing this, we experience a complete life, even during times of trials we find comfort, joy, and peace.

Mom displayed her unconditional love to me. She did exactly what she was supposed to do here on earth. She always protected, always trusted, always hoped, and always persevered.

Celebrating at the beach with family—10th Anniversary

I Found Love

Veronica and Jason—10th Anniversary

I finally understood what it was to honor my parents, which is to live a good life, the good life Mom would talk about, which is to live a life of LOVE. Mom didn't tell me about love, she showed me love, and even though she's now gone, I can still experience that kind of love, because God gives it to me, and shows me His complete and unconditional love daily.

God continues to light my path and leads me as I surrender my life to Him daily. He allows me to be who I am and continues to shape me into more of the woman He created me to be. He is my true love, joy, song, strength, rock, and the inspiration of my heart. I am His and He is mine.

I know today that no matter what, He will never leave me or forsake me. He says that to me in Deuteronomy 31:6. I understand that no human being will ever complete me. I'm already complete in Him.

I'm blessed with the chosen husband for me. God chose this man for me. Jason is my one. He is always my first encourager and cheerleader who has believed in me and accepts me for who I am.

When Mom met Jason, she said to me that he would make a good husband and that his family would love me. I wish she could have seen it for herself. I am thankful for the mercy of God that allowed her to see it before I could even see it for myself. She was right about that.

Jason not only gave Mom hope, but he gave her the gift of seeing her daughter read God's word to her. I would always read the Bible to Mom while we both soaked the warmth of the sun in May's backyard. Mom and I shared a favorite book in the Bible—Proverbs. I now see God's tender and handy work in all of my life. God knew Mom's desires as well as mine. Before Mom left this earth, God allowed her to see His unending love for her, and He gave her endurance, strength, comfort, hope and peace.

Jason, my loving husband, is a caring dad to our children. He loves me and my family. I have so much gratitude for this man. My love for him grows each day I grow older with him. I love his protection, leadership, honesty, and the love he has for our family. I know he is a gift from God. God's perfect gift for me. Jason is the man I get to love for the rest of my life. He is now the one in my life who is loving me here on earth the way God wants him to love me and as he grows in God's love, I and all who know him benefit from it. Jason helps me be a better person and it's because of him, this book was written. He always said,

"Vero, you should write your story."

It all started as a thought years ago, when one day Jason called me from work and asked, "What would be one thing you'd want to do if you were given an opportunity?"

I laughed and said, "I would like to go to wine tastings whenever I want."

He laughed but said, "OK, I get that, but seriously, what would be one thing you would want to do? Think about it."

After thinking about it, I decided that one thing I had always thought about doing was to write my story. Jason always encouraged me to do exactly that.

I said to him, "Well, I do like to write a lot of my thoughts, feelings, and prayers and I think I'd like to start writing my story so that I can leave it behind for my kids."

Jason immediately said, "Okay, I have a laptop here at work for you to use. I will bring it home today."

He brought the computer home and placed it on top of the kitchen counter. The computer sat there for days. I was reminded every morning for about two weeks that I should start writing my story.

When the kids were in school, I would take a couple of hours to concentrate and travel back to my past. I would write each day until I needed to pick up my kids from school. Jason would always encourage me to just write and not worry about how perfect my wording was and only to write my thoughts and feelings. He would always tell me we'll both go back to review and make corrections if we needed to.

I wrote, wrote and wrote, and the more I wrote, the lighter I felt. I wasn't just writing, but I was healing, too. I discovered that I knew myself more than when I started writing.

I am so grateful that I listened to my soul, my husband, and God's voice, because when I did, I discovered that God had always been there with me. He gave me my very own heart's desires, a vibrant and young husband. He gave me two beautiful sons and a beautiful daughter that I love very much, so much that words can't explain the love I have for them. I get to experience God's love and beautiful blessings daily. He gave me back what the locust tried to take from me—Joel 2:25.

I wake up every day, loving what I have, and feeling overjoyed and complete in Him. I wake up to hear my husband say that he loves me, loves my face, and tells me that he knew my face would always be naturally beautiful in the mornings, even without makeup. He says that I don't need makeup but that he understands it's a girly thing. But that's not the only thing he loves about me. He says the most important things he loves about me are my heart and laughter, and that the heart is what matters because beauty fades away, but the heart never does.

It reminds me of Mom who wanted us to be beautiful inside, and out.

My kids tell me I'm the "best mommy in the world" and they tell me they love me so much. When I hear these words coming from their young mouths, my heart explodes with gratitude for these sweet souls I've been blessed with. I wouldn't trade anything in the world for this and in the end, it has all been worth it.

I feel like the most loved wife and mother in the world. I'm only true, honest, and real because of Him who fills me with His love. God has given me permission to continue to be who He has made me to be. I don't have to second guess myself or feel afraid of being judged by others. I don't have to change for anyone, but only for Him, as he continues to grow me. I know I'm who I'm supposed to be, and I am exactly where I need to be today.

I will continue to trust in Him all the days of my life. I can rest, rejoice, and know that I won't ever have to feel alone. I know He will always be there to hold me and comfort me during times of trials. He already has done this, even when I couldn't see him. He has always been by my side. He has blessed me with His love and this life that I now have. God never gave up on me. He put the right people in my life to lead me onto His path of love, hope and completeness.

I am grateful for them as well as for those people who weren't always loving to me but served a purpose to lead me on the path I am still on. I learned what love is and what love is NOT.

Jason and I know that there is something bigger and higher than ourselves. We believe that we were put together by God's own design. We know that He's the one who makes our love and marriage stronger every day. We also know that only with Him, our marriage will endure. In Him, we put our trust. In Him is our hope and with Him we will continue to persevere. God's plans are best! We both know this and surrender to His will. I will look up to Him all the days of my life. With Him I will persevere to the finish line.

I tell Jason and the kids that I will live to be one hundred years old. He says I will live longer than that. But my Father

God already told me when I'll be going home. It'll be when I am finished doing what He has placed me on this earth to complete.

My prayer is that His love, light, and hope will continue to be seen by many, even after I am gone. I will leave knowing that my job here has been done and I will go home to meet my Abba, Father! God's peace will reign over me forever and He will be there waiting for me where everlasting LOVE, JOY and PEACE resides.

Love always protects, always trusts, always hopes and always perseveres.

His love never fails—1 Corinthians 13: 4-7.

"I FOUND LOVE, LOVE IS GOD!"

For whoever finds me, finds life, and receives favor from the LORD—Proverbs 8:35 (NLT)

> The Lord is my Shepherd;
> I have all that I need.
> He lets me rest in green meadows;
> He leads me besides peaceful streams.
> He renews my strength.
> He guides me along right paths,
> bringing honor to his name.
> Even when I walk through the darkest valleys.
> I will not be afraid,
> for you are close beside me.
> You're rod and your staff
> protect and comfort me.
> You prepare a feast for me,
> In the presence of my enemies
> You honor me by anointing my head with oil.
> My cup overflows with blessings.
> Surely your goodness and unfailing love will pursue me
> all the days of my life,
> and I will live in the house of the Lord
> forever.
> Psalm 23:1-6

I Found Love

The Bornn Family

ACKNOWLEDGMENTS

I acknowledge the following:

All those souls who came before me and who sacrificed much for me to have the life I have today.

Susan Bornn, for loving me like her own daughter.

Jason, for your love, support, and for protecting our marriage, and my heart.

Chandrika David, for being a generous, wonderful friend, prayer warrior, and writing a beautiful and encouraging foreword.

Coco for being my fake twin sister; without you, I wouldn't be here. I am so grateful for living a life having you so close to me.

Pastor Pete Van for leading me to Christ with his powerful message on that first day I stepped into the church.

Pastor Rusty George for taking the time to review my book and for writing an amazing foreword.

Stacy Dietz, for blessing me with coaching to become a spiritual mentor, and for taking the time to review my book.

Tina Gardener, for being a true, loving, supportive friend to me; and for being my soul sister.

Apolonia Hopkins, for being a prayer warrior for me.

Carina, my baby sister, thank you for helping me dig up some of Mom's beautiful stories.

To the rest of my brothers, for blessing me by being part of my life growing up.

Willa Robinson, for really capturing my idea and voice for this book.

Frank, and all the rest, who have made my dream of publishing this book, become a reality.

My OOI and OOII Ladies and prayer warriors, I love you from the bottom of my Corazon.

ABOUT THE AUTHOR

Veronica Bornn is an accomplished woman who has used her vast life experiences to learn and grow into the woman she is today. She was a student of the Titus Women's Bible study, where she learned more of God's love and purpose for her life from some amazing women. After this, she participated in a Women's Mentoring Program at Real Life Church of Santa Clarita, California, where she served as a Mentor for several younger women. Following this, she went on to participate in IBSF (International Bible Study Fellowship) as a student first and then a leader for the first Spanish speaking woman's group. She enjoys hospitality and sharing time with family and friends.

Veronica is currently an elementary school safety supervisor after being a stay-at-home mother for 18 years. She lives with her husband of 21 years and their three teenage children in Santa Clarita, California.

AFTERWORD

Veronica wrote this book more than ten years ago. Jason and Veronica recently celebrated their 21st wedding anniversary. Their oldest son is a freshman in college, the middle son is entering his senior year of high school, and their youngest daughter is entering her sophomore year of high school. Jason and Veronica love date nights, going to the beach, traveling, cooking, eating, wine tasting, reading, walking, biking, and caring for their children, friends, family, and two little Shih Tzu dogs. They both continue to grow individually and surrender their lives to Christ daily.

Pablo is happily married living in Utah with his beautiful wife, the older son, and grandson, while his younger son is in the Army, married with three boys, and stationed in New York. Victorio served his time and was released after ten years in prison. Adan was denied release time after time, but never lost hope, bettered himself, and continued believing. After 24 long years, finally, he was granted freedom.

www.ingramcontent.com/pod-product-compliance
Lightning Source LLC
Chambersburg PA
CBHW072027110526
44592CB00012B/1419